ST. MICHAEL'S SEMINARY & NOVITIATE
OF
THE NORBERTINE FATHERS
1042 STAR ROUTE, ORANGE, CALIFORNIA 92667

ABOUT THE AUTHOR

Bishop Fulton J. Sheen was born in El Paso, Illinois. He was educated in schools in Illinois and is an *Agrégé en Philosophie* of Louvain University in Belgium. Following his studies at Louvain he taught in England for a year. He was then assigned to the Catholic University in Washington, D.C., where he became famous as a teacher. His sermons on the radio program *The Catholic Hour*, which he inaugurated in 1930, brought him national prominence. In the fall of 1952, he gave up radio for his own television program, *Life Is Worth Living*. He became a monsignor in 1934 and was consecrated Auxiliary Bishop of New York in 1951. He was named Bishop of Rochester in 1966. As National Director of the World Mission Society for the Propagation of the Faith, he supervised the writing and editing of all the Society's literature. He is the author of more than fifty books and a nationally syndicated column.

Books of Bishop Sheen's which are available in Image Books are *Peace of Soul, Lift Up Your Heart, The World's First Love,* and *These Are the Sacraments.*

The Power of Love

Fulton J. Sheen

IMAGE BOOKS

A Division of Doubleday & Company, Inc.
Garden City, New York

Image Books edition 1968
by special arrangement with Simon and Schuster, Inc.

Image Books edition published February 1968

The lines from "Do I Love You Because You're Beautiful?" are copyright © 1957 by Richard Rodgers and Oscar Hammerstein II and reprinted by permission of Williamson Music, Inc., New York.

Nihil Obstat: Edward J. Montano, S.T.D., Censor Librorum.
Imprimatur: Francis Cardinal Spellman, Archbishop of New York.
July 28, 1964

Copyright © 1964 by Maco Corporation, Inc.
Copyright © 1965 by Simon and Schuster, Inc.
All rights reserved
Printed in the United States of America

*Dedicated
to
the "Love we just fall short of in all love . . ."
and
the "Beauty that dost leave all beauty pain"*

CONTENTS

THE TRIAL OF LOVE

President Kennedy, R. I. P. 13
The Aftermath of an Assassination 15

THE NATURE OF LOVE

Liking and Loving 19
Three Words for Love 21
Those Who Love 23
Love Is a Messenger 25
The Experience of Love 26
Because I Love You 28
Projection 30

LOVE AND SELF

The True Orbit 35
Selfishness 37
Self-Abandonment 41
Loneliness 43
The Unknown Self 46
Introspection 48
Finished Living 49
Happiness 51

LOVE AND SOCIETY

Speculative Benevolence 57
Foreign Aid 59
Little Things 61
Courtesy 63
Sympathy 65
Identification 69
Judgment 71
True Giving 73

LOVE AND MARRIAGE

Castles in Spain 77
Love and Reality 79
Modern Woman 81
The Progression of Love 83
Evolution 85
The Crescendo of Love 87

LOVE AND CHILDREN

What Children Are Like 91
Guilt 93
Guidance 95
Children and Obedience 97
Teen-agers 99
Youth and Morality 101
Being Thankful 102

THE POWER OF LOVE

The Meaning of Life 107
The Ultimate Appeal to Virtue 109
The Mystery of Suffering 111
Those Who Suffer Persecution 113
The Meaning of Death 115
The Right Kind of Optimism 117

INTRODUCTION

Love is like liberty—it can be misused.

Never stopping to think what life would be without it, we take it for granted. Even the verb "to love" is used so casually that its meaning is dissipated.

Love has many shades of meaning, many layers of depth. It is a mirror revealing the character of the one who loves. It is born of a need and a sympathy, and it involves body and soul.

To understand its power, one must realize that love does not mean to have, to own, to possess; but to be had, to be owned, to be possessed. It is not the using of another for the sake of self, but the giving of self in order to help another. For one who lives in isolation, love becomes selfishness.

Love is not a circle circumscribed by the ego; it is more like open arms serving humanity. Practically every psychotic person is an egotist. He refuses to put aside self for the sake of another. On the other hand, the most normal people are those who measure life not by the wine that is drunk, but by the wine poured forth—in the good that is expended on others.

God loves everybody, not because everybody is lovable— but because He puts some of His own love into each person. That, in essence, is what we have to do: put some of our love in others. Then, even an enemy becomes lovable.

Love itself starts with the desire for something good.

Without this desire, there can be no love of any kind. Through love, every heart seeks to acquire the perfection or the good that it lacks, or to express the perfection it already has. This goodness is not always moral goodness; it can be physical or it can be utilitarian. But there is not one single area of life that is not affected in some way by love.

If one loves, everything is easy; if one does not—everything is hard.

As the smallest light beam is but a reflection of the light and heat that are the sun, so all truth and all love have their origin in God.

Love, indeed, makes the world go round—and takes it back to its ultimate source, which is God.

The Most Reverend Fulton J. Sheen, D.D., Ph.D.

The Trial of Love

PRESIDENT KENNEDY, R. I. P.

A YOUNG WOMAN leaning over the bloodstained body of her spouse is the picture of the world's greatest tragedy. It recalls that moment when the crimsoned body of Christ was taken from a Cross and laid in Mary's lap.

In all the heartbreaking dramas of the world, a woman is summoned to have her heart pierced mystically, as a man's heart is riven with steel. A Jacqueline leaning over a John is a compassionate beating of a heart in rhythm with a Mary leaning over a crucified Jesus. Grant the infinite distance between a God-man dying for the sins of the world and a man dying because of a man's inhumanity to man; grant that unbridgeable span between voluntarily laying down one's life and having it violently taken away—the latter still derives its value from the former, as the coin from the die.

I was in Rome in the first shattering shock of the death of President Kennedy. The suddenness of his death came like an earthquake; it affected so many and in such magnitude that one could not find a heart to console—others, too, were inconsolable. In lesser bereavements, there are those who are not involved, but then there were no others to wipe away tears, for they too were mourners.

Nothing is as democratic as death, for all of a sudden, there is no distinction between Jew or Greek, male or female, socialist or totalitarian, Republican or Democrat. All suddenly realize the wickedness of the world in which we live. Not until we see what is done to the humanity-loving do we grasp the frenzied hate which will not be stilled by the tears of a little John or the whimpering sadness of a Caroline.

Everyone says: "The world has lost a great leader." True! But in the future, we may speak of "our Second Emancipator."

It takes a sacrificial death to break down the walls of division. When some men refuse to acknowledge others as their equals under God, words will not unite them. It takes blood. It took a Lincoln's blood to unite a nation; it has taken a Kennedy's blood to prepare for the equality of men in that same nation. This is the mystery of his death—the price men destined for greatness have to pay to prove that love is stronger than hate.

Dorothy L. Sayers, thinking about God taking upon Himself the hunger, thirst, anxiety, fear, and sins of men, wrote: "The Christian Faith is God taking His own medicine." To saints, missionaries, nurses, and to others is sometimes given the vocation to let the sufferings of their fellow man pass through the channel of their common heart—and it breaks.

Only twice, perhaps, in the history of our nation has the desire to unite men in peace made presidents take on themselves the burden of human inequality to a point of saving others at the cost of self. On a brighter Easter day, we shall see that our national brotherhood was purchased by the blood of a victim—John Fitzgerald Kennedy. In the future, too, at the other end of a pool where the image of the victim Lincoln is reflected, there will be cast another monument, the heroic image of the victim Kennedy, for both were great, not by what was done *by* them, but what was done *through* them.

He has crossed the "New Frontier," that mysterious dividing line where a man goes to render an account of his stewardship. He need not fear, for "Blessed are those who suffer . . . in the cause of right." Lincoln's death gave us peace for decades afterwards. May God grant, through the same Calvary-Law of sacrifice in President Kennedy, that peace "which the world cannot give."

Above all our national figures, these two Presidents of Sorrow stand forever near the Man of Sorrows saying: "I will stand here at Thy side; despise my nation not."

THE AFTERMATH OF AN ASSASSINATION

PERHAPS we never thought of it before, but underneath our grief was the surprising truth that we measure the enormity of a crime by the nobility of the victim. The same act committed against a fellow citizen would have been murder too, but it would have convulsed us more if the mayor of a city were killed in identical circumstances; and still more if it had been the governor of a state. The top of the tottering pyramid of grief is reached when the president of a nation is assassinated.

The impact, the scandal, and the paralysis mount with the eminence of the one slain. Thus, suddenly, without our ever having suspected that we knew any theology, we affirmed in grief that principle that "Sin is always measured by the one sinned against." I will not carry it any further than to say: Suppose that Perfect Innocence and Truth and Love became a victim to evil and mediocrity, and was put to death by us? Would not our grief be almost too deep for tears?

Thus the murder of a president has suddenly made us realize that Dallas is not far from Calvary, that the death of the head of a nation has in it some reflection of that sorrow for the death of the Head of humanity, and that even in our democratic world, in which we tend to level off all things, we still have in our souls a hierarchy of grief. The nobler the victim, the greater the sin, and the deeper the grief.

We have walked with pleasure for many a mile and we have smiled and smiled, and learned nothing. But what a vista of the mystery which lies in the heart of the world's redemption was unveiled when we, as a people, walked with sorrow!

People become more united in sorrow than in pleasure. This is the second lesson learned in the dark pages of our national loss. Across the nation, citizens were enjoying theaters, sports, parties, cocktails, and a thousand and one pursuits of eros in which the ego satisfies itself under the guise of a love of another. Then all these disparate and separate enjoyments, like scattered drops of mercury, suddenly came together in one center—the broken heart of America. There were no longer political parties, business competitors, grasping fingers—there was beating only one heart.

What was the mystery behind it all? Again, without knowing any theology, we became theologians. We suddenly realized that we were actors in another drama: "In the death of One Man, all die." We died with President Kennedy because our human nature has already been stamped with that Value whence all values derive: in the death of the Lord we all die, and in His resurrection, we all live. Strange it is how human nature, forgetting its faith, suddenly is illumined by it. Why, not only Americans, but the world—all humanity—was made one! We should have remembered it without a murder.

As quick as a rifle shot, he who said that we are debtors to our country gave that which signifies the fullness of all giving—the surrender of life, human love, and lawful power. He who said that we should all be as creditors to our country now signed a receipt of patriotism which read: "Paid in full." Giving takes on some value because there was once Divine Giving which, across the debt of sin, wrote: "Paid in full."

It is well to be proud of our country, but if the memory of a death means anything, we will no longer boast as if the peacock were our national symbol, saying: "I am an American," but, in the full consciousness that our symbol is an eagle mounting ever upwards, we will say: "May I be worthy to be an American."

The Nature of Love

LIKING AND LOVING

It is not easy to like certain people, but it is possible to love them. The difference is this: Liking is instinctive, emotional, organic, physiological, a sensible reaction over which sometimes we have as little control as over the grumbling of a stomach. Arguments are useless in convincing a boy he ought to like spinach. When Herbert Hoover was President, the young son of a congressman was invited to dinner. The President ordered a menu boys like, such as chicken, ice cream, and cake. The cook, on his own, added spinach. The boy later on told his companions that he ate dinner with the President and he recounted the menu. His friends would not believe him, because a president does not have to eat what nobody likes, and nobody likes spinach. It took a letter from the President to convince the other boys that he did sit at the President's table—even though spinach was served.

But loving is in the will, not in the glands; it is in that part of our being which is subject to moral command, and is not a bodily reaction, like a wink. Hence, though we do not like certain medicines, we can put ourselves under the dictate of the will and take them. Liking is reciprocal, but love is not necessarily reciprocal. The friends we say we like, like us. But a mother can love a wayward son even though he does not return the affection. God can love us even when we spurn His graces.

The Divine Command was not "like thy neighbor" but "love thy neighbor," because it is hard to like certain kinds of people, such as those who step on our toes or make funny noises when they drink soup. But they can be loved, at the beginning, sometimes only by a good deed done to them. That is why the urgency to love thy neighbor is followed by the command: "Do good." At first it may be very difficult when our feelings are contrary to the command, such as telling a six year old boy: "Now, go out and kiss your Aunt Sophie." But doing good deeds which love demands makes the heart warmer. When there is no spontaneous love, love begins only as a duty. But as we learn to write by writing, to cook by cooking, to be courteous by practicing kindliness, so we learn to love by loving. The "I ought" after a while passes to "I love."

This becomes clearer as we grasp the mystery behind "love thy neighbor as thyself." First of all, the neighbor is not the one next door, or the one who borrows sugar. The neighbor is the one in need, or maybe even an enemy. But how can he be loved as I love myself? Well, how do I love myself? Do I love myself always, or at certain moments? Do I love myself when I do something embarrassing, or when I steal, or when I hurt my neighbor's reputation? On the other hand, do I not love myself when I visit the sick, send money to lepers in Asia, or find a job for the father of a family?

When analyzed, it becomes clear that I love myself when I do what is good, and I hate myself when I do what is wrong. There will be certain things in my neighbor which I love, and other things which I will not love, and they are the same things that were loved and hated in me.

Applying it in a general way, I will love the sinner, but hate the sin; love the thief, but hate the robbery; love the Communists, but hate Communism. The Church, therefore, will always accept the heretic back into the treasury of her souls, but never the heresy into the treasury of her wisdom.

It is easy to like and love those who love us. But when it comes to loving those who are not very likable, it takes the love of God to give the inspiration. Socialism is the love of neighbor without the love of God; it is the organization of society on a technical, scientific basis, rather than charity. Love is not love unless it is directed to a person. Every human being ought to be loved in the unique mystery of his concrete personality. And when we come across many persons whom we do not "like," then we have to do what God does with us, who are not very lovable; He puts His love in love, and thus finds us very lovable.

THREE WORDS FOR LOVE

In English there is merely one word for love; if there are synonyms, they do not have very definite shades of meaning. For example, "I love Paris in the springtime," "I love crepes suzette," "I love Mary," all use "love" indifferently. Rightly has it been said that the Greeks had a word for it—in fact, they had three.

The first word for love was "Eros," which is generally what is meant by sex-love; it is something biological, glandular, instinctive, emotional. It does not always distinguish between the pleasure and the person. Too often the wine can be drunk and the glass forgotten. The illusion is created that there is deep affection for the other person, but what really happens is that the ego is projected into the other person. What is actually loved is the pleasure which the other person gives. The frosting on the cake is eaten but the cake is ignored.

This erotic love sometimes turns to hate. This could never be if the other person were really loved, because love would exist whether the other person reciprocated love or not. When the ego feels that it no longer is receiving the pleasure it expected, there develops a contempt on the grounds that one has been "cheated." This is a very immature kind of love and that is why its sponsor, Cupid, is generally pictured as a child that has never grown up. When one reads of a divorce after a few years of married life, one can be sure that it was an erotic love which was at its basis. As a Russian writer has so well put it: "If unreciprocated love is hard on the heart, sometimes reciprocated love can be worse."

The second Greek word for love is "philia." This is the kind of love which exists both in friendship and in marriage.

In erotic love, the other person is replaceable; in philia, the other person is irreplaceable. No one can take the place of an intimate friend, of a devoted wife, or a consecrated mother. Philia is based on some kind of community of feeling, interest, or service; the intellect rather than the glands dominates the affections; the relation existing is that of an I-thou relationship rather than the I-it relation; affection is based on the responsibility of the I for the thou. This was the kind of love that Damon had for Pythias, that made Jacob serve seven years to win the heart of Rachel, that a wife has for a husband such as is expressed in the poem of Elizabeth Barrett Browning, the last lines of which read:

> . . . —*I love thee with the breath,*
> *Smiles, tears, of all my life!—and, if God choose,*
> *I shall but love thee better after death.*

The third word for love was not much used in classical Greek; it was a love so noble and divine that Christianity alone made it popular—that word is "agape." It was used only ten times by Homer; it is found only three times in Euripides; later on, it was used a bit in the popular Greek which was spoken throughout the world after Alexander conquered it. The Greeks did not need such a word, because Plato held that there could be no real love between God and man, inasmuch as the gods being perfect desired nothing; therefore, they had no love for man. Aristotle argued in the same way. He said that there was too great a disproportion between man and God to have any love between the two.

When God sent His only Son to this world to save it, and when His Divine Son offered His life on Calvary to redeem it, then was born a love between God and man which the Greeks could not and did not understand. That kind of love was best expressed by "agape." In contrast to it, the word "Eros" is nowhere found in the New Testament; the word "philia" in all its forms is found forty-five times, but the word "agape" is found 320 times. Once this agape began to exist, then it flowed down to illumine even the Eros; Eros became the sensible expression of the Divine Love; fraternal and friendly love was also sanctified by the agape inasmuch as we were to regard everyone else as better than ourselves. The only true lovers or friends are those whose love is explained by the agape of Him who so loved the world He sent His only begotten Son to redeem it.

THOSE WHO LOVE

ONE CAN never love in a hurry. Those who are particularly committed to loving service are the clergy and the doctors. To hurry the distressed and the disturbed, either through the confessional or the parlor or the clinic, is to make oneself a merchant dealing with things, rather than a dedicated servant of the poor, the sick, and the disturbed.

Love requires three terms, not only the lover and the beloved, but also that mysterious bond uniting both, which is love. Such human love reflects the Divine Love where there is an endless cycle of love in the Godhead. Every human person has within himself a rhythm or a tempo, to which the one who serves must tune in. To love means to be considerate of others; it may never be a carnal aggressiveness which seeks to devour the prey and be glutted; rather, it means listening to others, putting oneself in their frame of mind, rather than critically analyzing what they have to say. The speeding up of confessions, the rushing through a consultation, or imposing one's own mind on others in counseling, are failures to love. To love anyone means to give one's talent, to give one's time, to give one's money; in a word, to become identified with the soul in crisis.

A tendency in human nature, particularly among the strong, is to despise weakness. Boswell, in his life of Johnson, often remarks how unimaginative he was toward the sufferings of frailer constitutions. Sometimes unbroken health incapacitates man for sympathy with his fellows and weakens his power of insight into other minds; it makes him anxious to dispatch the burdens of others, as if they were wholly of their own making.

Love is patient, tolerant, benevolent. It extends to those beyond our own set, and is exercised not only to the good, but even toward the dull and the foolish who stumble. But to be patient with them requires that kind of love which sees in every single person an immortal soul, more precious to the Lord than the universe itself. No doctor and no clergyman can do anything for a man whom he dislikes. Medicine and theology prosper only in love.

Though we cannot love the weaknesses of others, yet we can love the weak and bear their infirmities, not breaking the bruised reed, nor quenching the burning flax. Infants are not cast out of doors because they cry and are troublesome.

Though Our Blessed Lord limited His public life to three years, one never finds Him impatient. Two of His greatest converts were made when He was tired. On His way to work one miracle, despite an interruption, He stopped to work another. Several times it is recorded of Him that He had no time to eat, indicating that He never hurried souls through their problems in order to fit His life into a routine. The one thing that He asked to be done in a hurry was the betrayal by Judas, as if to indicate that that kind of speed and impatience belongs to the work of evil.

The parable of the lost sheep is the story of long, patient searching; when the sheep is found, it is put upon the finder's back; it is not returned to the sheepfold by dogs nipping at its heels. The attitude of the one who finds the sheep is described as "rejoicing." As the Good Shepherd found all His care centered upon the lost sheep, so He now finds all of His joy flowing from it. Not only the lost sheep, but even the Cross rested upon His shoulders as a lesson to men that not only the wanderers but even the burden of the world's guilt is to be assumed by those who love.

LOVE IS A MESSENGER

LIFE IS FULL of invisible meanings or mystery. Love itself is a mystery. A mystery has two sides: one material, the other spiritual. One is seen, the other unseen. A handshake is more than the clasping of two hands. For example, if we put one of our hands inside the other, we do not regard it as a handshake. And why? Because there is lacking the invisible spiritual significance of friendship. A word is a mystery: there is more to it than a sound, for a dog could hear the sound as well as the human ear; rather, there is the invisible meaning. Words and handshakes, then, are messengers of things unseen; they tell a story of something else. An engagement ring is a messenger. It tells the story of a pledge of love. Beyond the material value of the ring is the invisible and unseen assurance of being loved. That is why the ring is placed on the finger which the ancients believed had a vein that led directly to the heart.

Of what is love the messenger? From whom does it come, and what is the message? Love is a messenger from God saying that all human affection is a spark from the great Flame of Love which is God.

Love is very much like the sunlight that bathes the trees of the forest, which in their turn sink into the earth and centuries later are dug up as coal. When they burn, they return again their debt of light from the sun. So the human heart, after burying love within, later on returns that love to the God from whom it came.

That love is a messenger is told in the veil which a woman wears on her wedding day. The veil is not, even among the Moslems, to make woman ineffective, nor to hide her personality; rather, the veil among all peoples is a symbol of the invisible. It is a sign that all has not been disclosed, that there are mysteries not yet sounded, treasures not yet discovered.

Love was meant to be a sign, a symbol, of the Divine. No man is the final goal of any woman, nor is any woman the ultimate purpose of any man. God is the end of both. Each person has the Infinite within him; it is that we are after. We are composed of body and soul. The body can reach a point where it has enough food and enough passion, but the soul never says "enough." All that we add are so many zeroes, none of which can satisfy until it goes back to the Infinite for which it was made. Only the universal can give us contentment, but all we find below is the particular. We want the garden and yet all we eat are little green apples. The Peace is in realizing that all human love is a spark from the Flame which is God.

In the natural order, God has given great pleasures to the unity of the flesh. But those are nothing compared to the pleasure of the unity of the spirit, when divinity passes out to humanity, and humanity to divinity.

If the human heart in all of its fine, noble, Christian riches can so thrill, can so exalt, and make us so ecstatic, then what must be the great Heart of Christ!

THE EXPERIENCE OF LOVE

MANY YOUNG PEOPLE who think they fall in love are actually falling in love with the *experience* of love. Because the other person gives a "glow," qualities are attributed to him or her which do not exist. She marries a "hero" and lives with a husband; he marries a "goddess" and lives with a wife.

Just suppose that while talking to you, I began tapping a pencil upon a table. You would notice it and perhaps consider that act strange. But if I did it every day, eventually you would not notice it. In order to bring it to your attention, I would have to pound much harder each succeeding day. This is an indication of how sensations and feelings wear thin. If, therefore, a marriage is based wholly upon feeling and emotions, then love dies when the emotion dies. But where there is a love of the person because of the nobility of character and goodheartedness, then love never ends, but increases from day to day. An old German proverb states: "When love is young, it bubbles like new wine; the more it ages and grows clear, the more it becomes still."

A young man may know and appreciate a number of young women, and yet in the depths of his soul remain unmoved. And then one day, a woman with no conscious purpose will release some secret spring in the depths of his personality, and from that moment on, she becomes the center of his world.

What creates this new condition? It may have been knowledge of her character and personality, but it may also have been spontaneous, or what is called "love at first sight."

One may ask if each of us does not really carry in his or her own heart a blueprint of the one that he or she loves. This blueprint is made by our reading, our prayers, our experiences, our hopes, our ideals, by our mother and father. Then, suddenly, the ideal becomes concretized and realized in a person, and we say: "This is 'it.'"

Each of us carries around in his own heart the music that he loves. We hear a certain kind of music for the first time, and we immediately love it. It satisfies the rhythm and the tempo that are already inside our hearts. Love at first sight may be incomprehensible, but it is a fact, nonetheless. In the end it may not be first sight; it may be just a dream coming true.

Beauty in a woman and strength in a man are two of the most common spurs to love. Physical beauty and vitality increase vigor in each other, but it is to be noticed that beauty in a woman and strength in a man are given by God to serve as purposes of allurement. They come at that age of life when men and women are urged to marry one another. They are not permanent possessions. They are something like the frosting on a cake or like the electric starter of an automobile motor. If love were based only on the fact that she is a model and he is a fullback on a football team, marriage would never endure. But just as the frosting on the cake leads to the cake itself, so too do these allurements pass on to greater treasures.

A wife, on being congratulated for having a very handsome husband, once said: "I no longer notice that he is handsome; I notice now that he has greater qualities."

BECAUSE I LOVE YOU

A POPULAR SONG has these expressive and inquisitive lines: "Do I love you because you are beautiful? Or are you beautiful because I love you?" The thought behind this is that the lover can enrich the qualities of the beloved and see in the beloved that which others miss. Love is blind, so it is said, but the blindness is not always in the lover, but sometimes in those who look on one whom someone else loves. The lover may be blind to faults in the heart on which his seal has been set but, more often, of the same person, others may say: "What does he see in her?"

The great philosophers of the Middle Ages enunciated all this in a dry but universal principle: "Whatever is received is received according to the manner of the one receiving it." For example, food laid on a rock is not received in the same manner as food laid on the tongue; a sunset seen by a cow is not the same as a sunset seen by a poet; a child is endowed with a thousand qualities of attractiveness and loveworthiness which escape the cranky old bachelor.

Applying this to what was said above, love is a kind of

vision; it allows a penetration of the character of another which at times far surpasses knowledge. The lover has a vision of beauty which is denied the one who hates. When love goes, often even the truly beautiful ceases to be beautiful. A husband who begins to love another woman will wonder why everyone else considers his wife so attractive. He has lost the eyes to see her loveliness because of something that has happened inside him; not only the eyes but also the heart can grow cataracts which distort vision, so that the beautiful may even seem ugly.

The music that we love is the music we already have in our hearts. The kind of music people enjoy depends upon their inner rhythm and harmonies and even discords. Those who have not found peace will like music that is agitated; those who are at conflict with themselves will prefer music with discords. The inner melody of the heart determines what the ear would like to hear.

If it be true that what others seem to us depends to some extent on our love, it also follows that the dispositions of our heart and mind can distort, disfigure, or make appear in its true loveliness the image of Christ. There is an apocryphal work of the second century, called the "Acts of John," which gives an inspiring portrait of the way Christ seemed to James and John when He first appeared to them. To John, Christ seemed more beautiful than He did to James. John said to him: "My brother James, your eyes must be dimmed by many sleepless nights we spent on the lake." A writer of the second century, who therefore was very close to the Apostolic thought, wrote: "There has come to us a tradition of this kind, concerning Him, that He appeared to each as he was worthy. And though it was He Himself, yet it was not so that He appeared to all; like as is written of the manna when God sent bread from heaven to the children of Israel, which adapted itself to every taste."

Such would have accounted for the difference in attitude between a John and a Judas. The Son of God must have looked very different to Judas, when he saw that His kingdom was not to be political, than He did to John, whose heart was always aflame with love. This did not mean that objectively the Saviour was really different; but it did mean that everyone received Him according to his manner of receiving. The sun shines on wax and softens it; the sun shines on mud and hardens it. There is no difference in the sun, but only in that on which it shines. There is no difference in Christ, but each one receives what he is capable of receiving. Egotisms, selfishness, hate, envy, and luxury will distort the image. It was this Our Lord meant when He said: "You will not come to Me . . . I can see you have no love of God in your hearts." Love can endow an unattractive creature with attractiveness, as the words from the popular song indicate, but here it is the reverse; Divine Beauty, being always attractive, is lovable only to those who want the best; but He is a discord to those whose hearts are already off the key of decency or goodness.

PROJECTION

ADORATION is not necessarily the same as love. Love is directed to a special person, but adoration is a projection to another of an ideal that exists within one's own mind.

Actually, what a young man wants when he projects or adores a human person is the love of God. Man has two sides: a purely human side which belongs to his body, and a spiritual, infinite side which belongs to his soul. Until he falls in love, man may be very much like ice. Ice is the same as water, but it does not possess all its properties until it is melted. Man, before he comes in contact with God, is something like ice; when he contacts God even remotely in love, he has added another depth to his being. It is this interior image of Divinity that is worthy of adoration which the lover projects upon the beloved.

The Nature of Love

The lover himself is not very conscious of what is going on inside of him. But he divinizes the beloved woman. She becomes an absolute, and he identifies himself with this absolute. In every fiber of his being, all of his thoughts, emotions, desires, converge upon that divinized object. When this happens, the lover is not loving himself, but unconsciously loving God, insofar as God is the perfection of his being.

Plato put it beautifully:

> Few souls have enough of this gift of recollection, but those who have, when they happen to perceive an imitation of the things that are above, they are beside themselves and cannot contain their emotion. As to the nature of what they are feeling, they can render no account of it, not knowing rightly how to examine themselves.

Adoration quickly loses its purity, because the Divine Image soon becomes identified with the real woman. What was an ideal now becomes very concrete, and he becomes more and more dependent on it, like a drug addict. His love is turned into a need, so that he becomes a kind of a slave.

But on the other hand, a woman could not be on the pedestal for a man's adoration unless she had some resemblance to the Divine Image in her.

One of the dangers of teen-agers falling in love too quickly is that they are falling in love only with its ideal or projection. When they grow older, love becomes much more specific. It could very well be that one always falls in love with an ideal, or what is built up by experience into an ideal. That is why there can be such a thing as real love at first sight in the sense that the person who is loved is the realization of a dream come true. The ideal, which is in the mind of the adorer, is spiritual, but the woman who is loved is material, concrete, sensible to the eyes and ears, and belonging to an external world from which the lover himself is detached.

Because one realizes the disproportion between the ideal and the fact, there can result a terrific sense of being disappointed in love.

Teen-agers who fall in love too quickly become enmeshed

in the emotional pleasure the other person gives, without ever having time to judge those other qualities of mind and heart which may fall very short of the ideal. One paints with the brush of the infinite the one that is idealized, but then discovers that time wears off the paint.

Love and Self

THE TRUE ORBIT

As MAN conquers outer space, he seems to lose the conquest of self. In direct proportion as he masters what is outside of him, he seems to become enslaved on the inside. He has more room in which to stretch his muscles; he has less room in which to expand his soul. His thoughts dwell on orbiting the moon; but he himself has no orbit, no one thing around which he revolves. He knows how to control the universe; he does not know how to control himself.

Modern man is losing his soul; perhaps, what is worse, he does not realize he has a soul to save. If he loses that, he loses everything--even the civilization in which he lives. Sixteen out of twenty-one civilizations that have decayed from the beginning of the world until now did not succumb or fall through attacks from without; they fell by attacks from within by decay of the spirit.

Why is it that juvenile delinquency is highest in countries that are the most economically developed; why are there more psychotics and neurotics among the overprivileged than among the underprivileged? Such considerations as these make more momentous than ever the question of the Lord: "How is a man the better for it, if he gains the whole world at the cost of losing his own soul?" What if he does send a beast circling the moon, while the beasts of passion and selfishness devour him from within? The world indeed has to be remade, but the world will not be remade until man himself has first been remade.

There are three levels on which a man may live: first, the physical or the material; second, the sensible or the carnal; third, the spiritual or the Divine. One corresponds to the feet, the other to the body, the last to the head. Communists have only feet. They can see nothing but materialism. Sensualists, who live only for pleasure or sex or for the satisfaction of their corporal needs, crawl on their stomachs. The spiritual man does not disdain either the material or the sensible, for he walks on his feet, cares for his body, but realizes that within him there is a hierarchy of values and all are subject to his head, to his spirit, and to his God-likeness. He is the master in his house; the others are the servants.

How does man establish this hierarchy within himself, making all material things serve his body and both of them serve the spirit? He does it by realizing that there is within him a dynamic power which is called love. Love is an expansion, a going out of self, in order to help the neighbor, either as family, or nation, or humanity.

This expansive love is absolutely impossible without a practical knowledge and love of God. First of all, what is the basis for loving all men regardless of race or color, if it be not the fact that God is the Father of all? It may be said that we can have a brotherhood of men. But is it not nonsense to say that men are brothers, unless they have a common father? To speak of the brotherhood of men without the Fatherhood of God is to make us all a race of illegitimate children.

Furthermore, if there is no example of the expansive Love of God, who came to this earth to save those who have sinned against Him, then what basis is there for loving those who hate us, and who do us harm? Our Blessed Lord, speaking of those who love the lovable, said: "What title have you to a reward? . . . Will not the very heathen do as much?" There is only one reason for loving those who apparently are not worth loving, and that is because we who are not worth loving are loved by God. It is only by meeting God that we meet men.

Is there any fun in motoring if we do not know the road? Is there any joy in building one's home if one does not have a plan? If man does not know why he is living, then what is the good of living? Water becomes a power only when it is harnessed; it vivifies only when it is canalized by irrigation. And all the powers of man—material, physical, sensual, intellectual—are unified only in terms of his ideal and his faith in God. It shows a great power over explosive nature to be able to circle dogs in orbit about the earth, but man will never be happy until he has been able to put the beast that is in him in orbit around his reason, around his faith, and around his God.

SELFISHNESS

THE WORLD would be very grateful to any psychiatrist who would make a statistical study comparing mental troubles and selfishness. Here it is assumed that the investigation would not concern itself with organic or physiological causes of mental troubles, but solely with egotism. It is interesting that in the English language the words "selfish" and "selfishness" were not known until about 300 years ago. Shakespeare certainly does not dwell upon the idea. Could it be that the recent advent of the word in history corresponds in some way with an increase of that which it describes? As a sin, selfishness is as old as man, and has always been identified as undue love of self. An unknown author described selfishness in the following poem:

> I had a little tea party this afternoon at three.
> 'Twas very small—three guests in all—just I, myself and me.
> Myself ate all the sandwiches, while I drank all the tea.
> 'Twas also I who ate the pie, and passed the cake to me.

Selfishness does not mean that there is not to be a proper love of self. Our Blessed Lord told us: "Love thy neighbor as thyself." Self He made the standard by which the neighbor is to be loved. This could not be, if love of self did not have a legitimate basis. Selfishness is the love of the wrong self; that is, the self that is indifferent to the feeling and the interest and the safety of others. Man is not selfish because he wishes to earn enough to raise his family, but he is selfish if he consults only his own gains regardless of the losses that he may bring on others.

Trench tells the story of an architect who was ordered by the King of Egypt to build a high tower which would warn mariners of the dangerous rocks in the sea. The architect cut in large letters in the stone of this tower, his own name. He then plastered over the carvings, and on the plaster in gold leaf wrote the name of the King, as if he were doing him honor. It was not long until the waves had washed away the plaster, and the only name that appeared was his own.

It is not unusual, therefore, to find that there are many who will apparently glorify others, even the King of kings, but in their own selfish way they are gratifying their own self-love.

All selfishness is necessarily unhappiness. The self is too small a prison in which to relax. Caring only for self is very much like a serpent devouring his own tail. There is a parable told in India that indicates how selfishness defeats itself. A selfish fool was bequeathed a rice field. The first season the irrigation water ran through his field and made it fruitful, then overflowed into the neighbor's field and gave him blessing. But the next season the selfish fool said within himself: "Why should I let all of this water flow through my field into his? Water is wealth, and I must keep it." He then built a dam which prevented the water from flowing into his neighbor's yard; but he found that he had no crop. The irrigation water brought blessing only as it flowed, and when it became stagnant it bred a marsh and a swamp.

The cure for selfishness is a generous overflowing of whatever self possesses, either to neighbor or to God. Rich people miss so much happiness in life by accumulating more wealth, rather than by visiting poor lands and individually helping the starving and the sick in those areas. The neighbor should be helped because he is another self; God will be thanked because all blessings come from Him. What a wonderful new world this would be if a psychiatrist would say to a patient stretched out on the couch before him: "Are you shifting to another a burden which you yourself should bear? Are you putting another to an inconvenience or trial in order that it may profit you? How many minutes of the day do you spend in helping your neighbor? How much money have you ever given to help the poor of the world? Have you ever thanked God that you have come to me that I might ask you these questions?"

Once I asked a missionary from one of the islands in the Pacific which was the greatest virtue of the people whom he helped there. He answered: "I can tell you their greatest virtue in terms of what they regard as their greatest vice, namely 'Kai-Po,' which is the sin of eating alone." Some of them would go without food for two or three days until they could find one with whom they could share their blessings.

In contrast, near a church in Warwickshire, England, is a stone on which is to be found the following inscription:

> Here lies a miser who lived for himself
> And cared for nothing but gathering pelf,
> Now where he is or how he fares
> Nobody knows and nobody cares.

On television recently there was an interview with a very rich man. Without any embarrassment, he said that he never gave anything to poor individuals, that he would stand on a sidewalk for a half hour hoping that some passerby would pick him up and he would not need to hire a taxi, and that in his magnificent home he had installed a pay telephone, in order that "my friends would not be embarrassed if they wanted to make a call."

Tolstoy told a beautiful story of a shoemaker who on the way home one night found a poor man shivering and poorly clad. Moved by pity, he took him home. But his wife complained about his bringing a stranger into the house and the cost of feeding another mouth. As she continued, the stranger grew smaller and smaller, shriveled and wrinkled with every unkind word. But when she spoke kindly to him and gave him food, he grew and became more beautiful. The reason was that the stranger was an angel from heaven in human form and could live only in an atmosphere of kindness and love.

The ungenerous soul has forgotten that everything he has came to him from God and that, acting as a trustee instead of an owner, he is one day to render an account of his stewardship. Furthermore, the more generous we are to others, the more merciful will be our own judgment. In driving home this lesson, Our Blessed Lord told the story of the one hundred sheep, the ten pieces of money, and the two sons—one of whom was a prodigal. One of the one hundred sheep was lost. Upon finding it, the shepherd put it on his shoulders and brought it into the house; the other ninety-nine were left in the field. The woman who had ten pieces of money rejoiced more at finding the one that was lost than in the possession of the nine which were safe. The father was so happy at the return of the prodigal son that he killed a fatted calf. These are pictures of the mercy, kindness, and the forgiveness of God to those who, in their turn, are forgiving, generous, and merciful.

At what point are selfishness and greed turned into thoughtfulness of others? In a limited way when we become conscious that all men are brothers. In a higher way through the realization that having the great debt of our sins forgiven, we seek to relieve the debts of others. Such was the inspiration of Zaccheus, a dishonest tax collector, who climbed into a sycamore tree to see Our Divine Lord. Our Lord told him that He wanted to visit his house. The Divine forces Himself on no man; He withholds Himself from no man. He respects that awful prerogative that each one is the architect of his own good or evil, by free and unrestrained choice. Immediately after the visit, Zaccheus, recalling all his dishonesty, promised to pay back all that he had stolen and, in addition, to give generously to the poor.

The one thing that makes a complete revolution in the soul of man, that changes selfishness into generosity, that upsets his value of the dollar and makes a new man of him is the manifestation of the supreme love manifested in God, who came down to this earth to pay our debt of sin and rescue us from the swamp of selfishness that makes us so weak and frustrated.

Today charity is organized, which means that many are pinched and approached and cajoled until they give. Pressure methods may get more in modern philanthropy, but there is no greater betterment of the giver or the receiver than when one gives because one has been forgiven; we love to increase the eternal content of love in the world.

SELF-ABANDONMENT

EVERY NOW and then in history, particularly in times of great spiritual and moral crises, an era of carnality erupts. There is an excellent description of this phenomenon in the letter that Paul wrote to the Romans in which he described the close relationship that exists between the rejection of God and homosexuality, and the rejection of authority with violence, and the primacy of sensate pleasure before duty. The latest figures reveal that persons under eighteen years of age were involved in 43 per cent of all the serious crimes in this country, and that youths under eighteen years of age were mixed up in 50 per cent of all burglaries, larcenies, and automobile thefts. In ten years, juvenile delinquency has increased 800 per cent. The United States has the largest narcotic market in the world.

Dr. Milton Senn, Director of Yale's Child Study Center, states that of all marriages in which both partners were high school students, there was a premarital pregnancy in 85 per cent of the cases.

This brings up the question: Are we suffering from a moral or a cultural degeneration? There is no doubt that it is a moral degeneration, but it involves more than youth. Therefore, it is a cultural decay. It often happens that an individual who is frustrated may look for some kind of escape in sexual promiscuity. So it is with society. When it runs up against a dead end, many aberrations, artistic, political, economic, and carnal, leave their sediment or scum on the surface of society.

Cultural decay reveals itself with society particularly in two areas: (1) public life, (2) family life.

In public life there is an evident want of integrity and honesty, in such things as the primacy of the "fast buck," price-fixing, built-in obsolescence in mechanical things, the substitution of the novel and the new for what is already practical and useful.

In family life, too, youth sees the wedding ring cut in two. Thirteen million youths in the United States are half-orphans. Some see drunken fathers, others see neurotic mothers. The want of fidelity and love in the home makes them as much despair of loyalty in private matters as honesty in public.

Parents will often say in justification of their position: "I can do nothing with my children." This is an absolutely correct answer, but it needs an explanation.

A mother who takes dope while she is carrying her child will see the child after birth suffer the effects of her own excesses. Somewhat the same symptoms of chills, "shakes," and other disorders pass into the infant. The mother in the face of the victimized infant may say: "I can do nothing for the infant." The fact is the mother has already done everything for the infant. She has made the infant that particular way. The blame is at her door, just as well as the blame for dishonesty and stealing in a boy is to be laid at the door of the father who cheated on his income tax.

Teen-agers, when frustrated in these two important areas of life, look for some kind of escape, and these are generally twofold:

1. There is produced a generation of beatniks, who are actually in protest against culture. They ridicule everything because they have no confidence in it. This ridicule expresses itself in the way they dress or fail to dress, in a general un-

cleanliness by which they manifest that they feel themselves as "strangers" to society and are characterless in a characterless society.

2. The other outlet is the orgiastic or the overemphasis on sex in which the youth tries to escape the decay of society by a return to the primitive, seeking a release in blood, though he can never find it, because he dresses it up in too sophisticated a manner. As a youth loves speeding, not in order to arrive someplace, but just for the excitement of speeding, so, too, a teen-ager is apt to turn to the carnal to make up for the loss of purpose in life and society and family by the intensity of an erotic experience. He seeks to destroy the mores which he knows to be corrupt and to drag everyone down to his own level. Abandonment becomes a substitute for creativeness. He hopes to receive back some compensation for what his sick soul has lost. Finding no home for the soul in the world, he becomes self-abandoned.

LONELINESS

T. S. Eliot wrote:

> *It isn't that I want to be alone,*
> *But that everyone's alone—or so it seems to me.*

One wonders if the modern dances of youth, in which they go through gyrations separately and without hardly ever looking at the partner, are not an indication of the terrible loneliness that possesses the modern soul in which each one is alone together.

There are various forms of loneliness: the loneliness of the child who, in moments of bitter isolation, feels unloved by parents; the loneliness of the boy who seems ostracized from the gang, or who is teased by the crowd because of some physical defect; the loneliness of the girl who feels like an island in a sea where everyone is prettier and more popular; the loneliness of the children of divorced parents, who spend the spring with one, the autumn with another, but it all adds up to a winter of discontent, tension, and frustration; the loneliness of the man who has passed middle age, and knows no other power than the biological which is already spent; the loneliness of the sinner, who feeds on husks as conscience tortures in the night, knowing that he should be living on the Bread of the Father's House; the loneliness of a man in power who is at the mercy of counselors who keep him more and more detached from common humanity whom he is destined to serve; the loneliness of the married who have exhausted all the subjects of conversation and who have forgotten to be companions in the wild pursuit of love; the loneliness of the unmarried who can dream of unending happiness that would have been theirs but have never put it to the test; the loneliness of the spiritually immature who have no one in whose presence they can take off the mask of sham and make-believe.

Tolstoy, at about the age of fifty, when he passed through what Dante calls "the middle of the journey of our life" or "the dark wood," described his loneliness: "All this took place at a time when so far as my outward circumstances went, I ought to have been completely happy. I had a good wife who loved me and whom I loved; good children and large property which was increasing with no pains taken on my part. I was more respected by my kinsfolk and acquaintances than I had ever been. I was loaded with praise by strangers; and without exaggeration, I could believe my life already famous. Moreover, I was not insane nor ill." But despite all of this, Tolstoy said that all on which he had built his life seemed to be a mockery. To his credit, however, it must be said that he found the answer.

Two remarks are in order concerning loneliness. One, it must not be thought that loneliness is always wrong. There is such a thing as detachment, retirement, escape from the crowds, a retreat, wherein one makes one's soul and prepares for action. Toynbee, in his *Study of History,* speaks of civilization being made by what he calls "a moment of withdrawal." The culture that concentrates solely on action and productivity exhausts itself. Before fulfilling destiny in quiet and peace, one must discover one's powers and come to a sense of mission. When the masses attempted to make Our Lord a king, He fled into the mountains alone. Before He chose His Disciples, He went into a mountain retreat and prayed. When the Apostles came back with a report of the success of their activity, He bade them retire into a desert place for contemplation. Before He began His mission or His public life, He went into the wilderness. It may, therefore, be that in the very heart of loneliness there is opportunity for spiritual growth and mental refreshment and enlightened vision. Loneliness may not be the terrible thing it is believed to be. Achievement can start in loneliness. Solitude can be very rewarding and full of blessing because in the silence of the inner being one finds God.

That brings us to the second point about loneliness—that it is terrible only where there is no faith, where this life is all, where the cup of passions which we thought would be filled endlessly is finally stained with dregs. When there is faith and the recognition that this life is the bridge to another, then lonely souls find an outlet in service and in doing something for neighbors. Lonely souls without faith generally take one of two outlets: they become aggressive and hate people, or they take flight from people and completely isolate themselves. Service begins when one realizes as John Donne put it: "No man is an island, entire of itself; every man is a piece of the continent, a part of the main . . ." It is not a question of going out into society, as much as it is of serving others. When the Lord asked "Dost thou love Me?" and received an affirmative answer, He then said: "Feed My lambs, . . . feed My sheep." Loneliness is overcome by praying for others, because when we pray for others, we begin to love them, and by serving others, it takes one out of the lonely ego and links one with the Love Which is God.

THE UNKNOWN SELF

IF WE WERE honest with ourselves, we would have to admit that each of us has more trouble with himself than with any other person in the world. We know other people better than we do ourselves. Someone once asked Socrates why he was such an unhappy man despite the fact that he traveled over the world. Socrates said: "Because wherever you go, you take yourself with you." The ancient Greek philosopher Thales said that for man to know himself is the hardest thing in the world.

The modern mind is completely surrounded by mechanisms for self-deception and for avoiding all knowledge of self. A mood is constantly being created that we are not personally responsible for the evil that we do. (It should be stated that, though many claim they are determined to be evil, nevertheless they insist that they should be praised for the good they freely do.) Another trick to avoid self-knowledge is exaggerated self-disgust. The victim thus affirms hopelessness and avoids the necessity of change. He says: "I am rotten," just as he might say, "I am too fat." Then he freely reaches for another chocolate. Sometimes one hears it said: "I am an old sinner." (They are always "old.") In such a false judgment one combines an affirmation of how sensitive is his conscience with the opposite affirmation that nothing can be done for his betterment.

The average person is very much like an onion; he is made up of many coats or disguises. Since tearing them off brings tears, he avoids stripping down to his real self. Many, too, are like icebergs—one-fifth of their character is above water, four-fifths is hidden and unexplored. Others are like depart-

Love and Self

ment stores in which the wrong price tags have been placed on many things: hairpins sell for $2,000; diamonds for a dime. Conscience they regard like bills at the first of the month—they are afraid to open them because they are bearers of bad news. Many a modern conscience is like a woman before her mirror. Just as soon as she sees herself, she puts on her makeup. The mask is made for others; the seeming self shows itself, while the real self is hidden. As Browning put it:

> *God be thanked, the meanest of his creatures*
> *Boasts two soul-sides, one to face the world with,*
> *One to show a woman when he loves her!*

Despite all these escapes, the real enemy is within. Man cannot love himself as he really is when he does wrong, so he blinds himself and tries to love the self that he *thinks* he is. The more proud a man is, because he knows little about himself, the more sensitive he is to the insults of others. But the man who knows himself, that is, not as he is before his own standards, nor as he is before his neighbor, but as he is before his God, that man is never much troubled about the attacks of others. His principal worry is himself, how he can become not just a man, but a child of God. A person will learn more about himself on his knees for five minutes than he will learn on a couch in five years—and it is much cheaper. Michelangelo had the right idea when he said: "Lord, take me away from myself to make me pleasing to Thee."

INTROSPECTION

NEVER BEFORE has there been so much probing, analyzing, searching, and introspecting of the human mind as in the present day. And yet we are all like children at the dentist. We protest the probing the minute it begins to hurt. As long as the analysis stays on the surface of the soul and does not touch self-complacency, we allow the search to go on. Like children at the seashore, we dig a little hole and boast that we "are digging to China," but in our heart of hearts we know that we never touch the depths.

The modern man is afraid of deeper experiences and is reluctant to be on terms of close intimacy with himself. From the message of the spiritual life he turns away as if it touched no secret spring in his heart. But in reality, it is a fear of ever being brought face to face with the real self which makes one shrink from the truth. Any religion is acceptable which allows man to continue the way he is. But a religion which brings him face to face with Heaven's standard makes the soul fear the probing.

And yet in the heart's depths there are spiritual aspirations, which are hard to quench. Pascal often seemed to hear God saying to him: "Thou couldst not seek Me had I not already found thee." The cry of the depths is more than human breathing; it is a Divine inspiration. The great obstacle to the communication between God and the soul is not ignorance; it is sin and evil. Because God is Love, He is ever coming down to the depths of life, sorrow, sin, and degradation in order to bring that soul to Himself by all the power of His Love.

Dr. Samuel Johnson said that he could not read without

profound emotion a line in a great medieval hymn: *"Tantus labor non sit cassus"*: "Let not all thy labors go for nought." Somehow or other, he wanted his aspirations of the soul to be caught up by the Divine, so that love's labor would not be lost.

Why try to escape from God? The Divine answer is "Men love darkness rather than light." The added tragedy of sin is that after we do wrong, we may not let God help us do what is right and good. We smash the bow so that He cannot play on our violin. We keep Him at arm's length because we refuse to be loved. We are drowning and will not clutch at His helping hand because in our pride we say that we must "work this thing out for ourselves." The truth of the matter is not that God is hard to find, but rather that man is afraid of being found.

In each heart there is a secret garden which God made uniquely for Himself. That garden is locked like a safe-deposit vault: it has two keys. God has one key and, therefore, the soul cannot let in anyone else but God. The human heart has the other key and, therefore, not even God can get in without man's consent. When the two keys of God's Love and human liberty, of Divine Vocation and human response meet, then paradise returns to a human heart.

FINISHED LIVING

THE MAN who does not believe in a future life has to take this one very seriously. He will never have another. But, if this world is a preparation for the next, then one can better enjoy both. Such a one does the little daily things of life, not for themselves, but for their purposes. He is like a climber on a rocky pathway who sets his foot upon each projecting point of stone, but who treads on each, not for its own sake, but for the sake of the one above it. The man who knows this life is not all does all the acts of today, but does them as if he did not do them, because he enters into a larger concept of life.

St. Paul says that those who weep should be as if they wept not and those that rejoice as though they had rejoiced not. By this he means we are not to be carried off our feet by either the troubles or the joys of life. We are not to make too much of either, but are to look beyond them to the purpose which God means them to serve.

Above all, we are to use the world, and in spirit still live as if we were not using it at all. The material exists for the sake of the spiritual. Everything in life is then seen as ministering to the glory of God. Our relationships with men thus tend to destroy selfishness. Temptations even reveal to us our weakness. The whole world is an arena of probation furnishing us with plastic material, the molding and shaping of which reveals our native royalty. As Tennyson wrote:

> *Life is not as idle ore*
> *But iron dug from central gloom,*
> *And heated hot with burning fears,*
> *And dipt in baths of hissing tears,*
> *And battered with the shocks of doom*
> *To shape and use.*

The world is designed to be a sphere of service for man and God. He who lives for the next one scores this one better. As the poet has said: "I could not love thee, dear, so much, Lov'd I not honour more." Think of what St. Francis has done for literature, art, love of animals, and simply because he loved none of these things as if they were final.

Our citizenship is in Heaven. We are here in an order to which we outwardly belong, but in the depths of our being we belong to another order altogether. The essential of Christian life, therefore, is to look forward to the city of Heaven, for here we have no continuing city, but live among transient, temporal things. This was the meaning of the Jewish Feast of Tabernacles, a reminder that we are pilgrims and we live here to complete our existence.

Most lives are like Schubert's *Unfinished Symphony*. They may also be compared to the statues of Day and Night carved by Michelangelo. Night is personified as a woman sunk in deep, yet uneasy, sleep; while Day is portrayed in the shape of a man who lifts himself in the attitude of wrathful and disturbed awakening. But the figure of Day has been left unfinished. The limbs are partly chiseled, while the head and face are merely blocked out of the marble. Some interruption stayed the master's hand. He left his work incomplete and a kind of parable of our human nature.

There is a pathetic sense of incompleteness about life, as there is in Day struggling to free itself from its stony shroud. But what a joy is his who can say at the end of life: "I have finished the work Thou hast given me to do."

HAPPINESS

IN DAYS when psychology takes the place of religion, self-aid supplants grace, psychoanalytic denial of guilt supplants pleas for forgiveness of sin, it becomes hard to realize that the great spiritual truths are really the reversal of all the world holds dear. Take, for example, the Beatitudes. While the world says: "Blessed is sex," the Beatitude teaches: "Blessed are the clean of heart"; when the world says: "Assert your rights, get your way," the Beatitude speaks of the happiness of the meek and the humble. When security and possessions are so much treasured, the Beatitude recommends the spirit of non-possession.

Happiness does not come to those who want to know all,

or to possess all, or to enjoy all; rather it comes to those who set limitations upon the satisfaction of self. A man, for example, cannot get the whole world into his hands, but he can wash himself of the world. Our powers of dispossession are greater than our powers of possession; there is a limit to what we can gain, but there is no limit to what we can renounce. In the end, the man who wants nothing is the man who has everything, for there is nothing that he desires. Our Blessed Lord expressed this truth in the gospel of Matthew 10:38: "He is not worthy of Me that does not take up his cross and follow Me."

To deny self is to refuse indulgence to lower desires, to put a restraint upon ourselves, to act differently from the way the sensual in our nature would lead us. Self-denial is the test of love, whether it be human or divine. The man who loves his business will deny himself, take up a cross of early rising, work late, just because he loves to make money. So it is with the love of God. An alcoholic would not prove that he loved God by swearing off soft drinks for life. In religion, many will follow God in prayer and even listen to His Word, but will not deny themselves their ease. There may be pain in self-denial for a moment, but pain in the pursuit of the highest is certainly more joyful than ease in the neglect of duty. The agony in self-denial is momentary, but the joy that flows from it is lasting.

> If you live a life of nature, you are marked out for death; If you mortify the ways of nature through the power of the Spirit, you will have life. (ROMANS 8:13)

John of the Cross, who lived 400 years ago in Spain, and was one of the greatest of all saints, was fond of writing poetry which contained sublime spiritual truths. All that has been written above in dull prose, he put in poetic lines:

> *To come to taste everything,*
>   *Do not taste anything.*
> *To come to know everything,*
>   *Do not seek to know anything.*
> *To come to possess all things,*
>   *Do not seek to possess anything.*

Love and Self

To come to what you do not taste,
You have to go where you do not taste.
To come to what you do not know,
You have to go where you do not know.
To come to possess what you do not possess,
You have to go where you do not possess.
To come to where you are not,
You have to go where you are not.
When you notice something,
Cease to throw yourself at everything.
To come from all to all,
You have to leave all for all.
And when you have come to have all,
You have to have it without wanting anything.

Love and Society

SPECULATIVE BENEVOLENCE

Some so-called kindly souls love the poor in theory, but not in practice. There is hardly any walk of life in which this spiritual deadness to the suffering of others does not exist. How many novels are written about sharecroppers, the unhoused, and the poor, but one wonders how much of the royalty earned from the story of the poor was ever returned to them. Some politicians who are rich feverishly plead for the underprivileged, but one wonders how many ever dug into their own pockets, or made an act of self-denial, or spontaneously raised the wages of any worker out of compassion for his distress.

This speculative benevolence is not beyond religion; a cripple mentioned in the Scriptures begged for years at the gate of the Temple, and received from passersby little more than scornful glances and pitiful pittances. Sheridan in his *School for Scandal* pilloried that type in these words: "As to his way of thinking, I cannot pretend to judge; for, to do him justice, he appears to have as much speculative benevolence as any private gentleman in the kingdom, though he is seldom so sensual as to indulge himself in the exercise of it."

Cornelius a Lapide tells how Thomas Aquinas called upon a churchman when he was counting money. "Do you see, Thomas," said the churchman, "the church can no longer say, 'Silver and gold I have none'?" Answered Aquinas: "Neither can the church say, 'Arise and walk.'" This story has reference to Peter and John entering the Temple and seeing the lame man begging alms referred to above. Peter fastened his eyes on him and John did too, saying, "Turn toward us."

The lame man, hoping he would receive something, actually heard Peter say only, "Silver and gold are not mine to give; I give thee what I can. In the Name of Jesus Christ of Nazareth rise up and walk." Taking him by his right hand, he lifted him up, and with that, strength came to his feet and ankles, and he sprang up and began walking.

These were two men, former partners in the fishing trade, who had their ecstatic hours of worship, but who realized that men cannot live in ecstasy nor apart from the need of man. Instead of keeping their piety speculative, they acknowledged the right of the lame and the afflicted to be heard and helped. Instead of giving a passing glance at social misery, it became to them a personal concern.

Lord Kelvin declared that he never understood a scientific principle in mathematics until he was able to make a model of it. During our twenty-five years as a university professor, we told students they never could say they understood anything, unless they could give an example of it. Neither can anyone boast that he has grasped the meaning of Christian charity, until he has put it in practice. Even where silver and gold are lacking, there is still room for faith.

Peter and John actually were giving less than others, and yet they gave more. They gave less materially, but gave more spiritually. It is not given to even the best of men of the twentieth century to work miracles, for miracles are like candles; they are used until the sun comes up. But though one cannot work miracles, one still can be a miracle in a world of selfishness by never disassociating love of the poor from prayer.

FOREIGN AID

FOREIGN AID is of the moment. Two great powers vie with one another in giving food to the hungry stomachs and parched tongues of the world. When one reads of the millions of dollars and rubles that are expended in this philanthropic work, one cannot help but recall a letter that was sent to the people of Corinth about aid, both foreign and domestic: "I may give away all that I have, to feed the poor; . . . if I lack charity, it goes for nothing." Note the contrast between giving and loving in the noblest sense of the word. Giving alone does not prove love; rather love manifests itself in giving.

The Jews, according to Maimonides, reckoned eight degrees of giving. The first was to give, but with reluctance and regret. The second was to give cheerfully, but not in proportion to the needs of the poor. The third was to give proportionately to the needs of the poor, but only after solicitation and request on the part of the poor. The fourth was to give, unsought and unsolicited, by putting the gift in the hand of the receiver in the presence of others, thus exciting in the poor a sense of shame. The fifth was to give in such a way that the poor would know who gave to them, but without the giver knowing it. Such was the case when money would be folded in the corners of the cloak, so that the poor who passed by might take it unperceived. The sixth was to give in such a way that those who received the gift never knew the giver. This was the case when an intermediary was used to send money to the house of the poor. The seventh was to give both unknowing and unknown, like those persons who deposited their alms in a poor box from which the poor were supplied without any ostentation or observation. The eighth, and the most noble of all the ways, was to anticipate kindness by preventing poverty, for example by paying the debts of another, finding him a job, educating him so that he is able to obtain livelihood without holding out an empty hand in beggary.

But none of these rose to the height of the charity envisaged by Paul, for to him, a man might give all his stocks and bonds to the poor, and have not charity; a nation might give millions to the impoverished peoples of the earth and have not charity; wanting this, one might swing a certain person or a nation into his own orbit, but in the Divine Ledger it would count for nothing. Love of God is inseparable from love of neighbor, otherwise there is apt to be much self-seeking. To give in order to make another nation our first trench in a war for our national defense is one thing; to give to another nation in order that people might be dispensed from material necessities to be free to lead virtuous lives and save their immortal souls is quite another thing.

Love that is above the natural is made the condition of entering the Kingdom of Heaven in that final judgment when motives for giving are judged. The people who are summoned to inherit the Kingdom are those who fed the hungry, clothed the naked, visited the sick.

The Judge of Hearts will say that in each instance it was He who was sick and hungry and in prison. The reason for making the exercise of this grace the test for heaven is because true giving springs from love. The open hand is the result of the religious heart. In the light of this, which nations will be blessed for foreign aid? Those who give to make people free on the inside because they have a soul and free on the outside because they have something they can call their own? Or those nations who give in order to win Fifth Columnists inside to stir up hate and a way of life which denies the soul on the inside and property on the outside? What Ralph Waldo Emerson said about helping others ought to be the inspiration of foreign aid by the United States: "When I have attempted to give myself to others by services, it proved an intellectual trick—no more. They eat your service like they eat apples, and leave you out. But love them and they feel *you*, and delight in you all the time."

LITTLE THINGS

AMERICANS are fond of using the words "greatest," "biggest," and "super," all of which indicate the tendency of mind to bow down before the statue of the Colossus, or before anything that is colossal. Grant the value of grossness and magnificence, may it still not be true that character resides in trifles and in the little things? Our Blessed Lord said that a drink of cold water given in His Name would not be without its reward. It will be noted that here the value does not reside precisely in what is small or little, but rather the motive for which it is given, or used. Beggars use tin cups; churches use plush-bottom collection baskets. The reason the beggar uses a tin cup is because he does not attribute a spiritual motive to the giver. He knows that the one who drops a dime loves to hear the jingle of his generosity. In the church, however, where gifts are offered out of love for the Lord, there is no echo that comes back.

Not the drink of water alone has merit, but the giving of it in the Divine Name, or with a spiritual intention. If we were to put on a scale, or a balance, what men regarded as the noblest gift which self-love could make, and on the other side of the balance, the most insignificant act or gift done out of love for Christ, we would find that the latter would far outweigh the former.

The difference between philanthropy and charity resides in this: Philanthropy is a gift without the love of God; charity is the gift with the love of God. Both the billionaire and the beggar can write checks for a hundred million dollars, but the former alone has value because of his name and the security that backs it up. Let then two equal gifts be given —one signed with one's own name, the other signed in the Name of Christ, and the latter has a worth that pierces Heaven. God does not weigh on the same scale as man. It was the widow in the Temple who gave the two smallest of coins, and yet, gave all she had, who was noticed by the Saviour. The small things indicate the store of Christian self-denial. Smiling upon a man in the hour of his defeat, as we bring to him the vision of the crown beyond the cross, reaching cups of cold water to parched lips in hospitals, as if the lips that touched the cup were those of Christ Himself— these constitute the ministry of small things to be remembered in eternity.

Oscar Wilde in his tragic book *De Profundis* tells us how unspeakably he was helped in his shame when a friend paid him the common courtesy of lifting his hat in his presence.

As Elizabeth Barrett Browning put it:

> What are we set on earth for? Say, to toil;
> Nor seek to leave thy tending of the vines
> For all the heat o' the day, till it declines,
> And Death's mild curfew shall from work assoil.
> God did anoint thee with his odorous oil,
> To wrestle, not to reign; and He assigns
> All thy tears over, like pure crystallines,
> For younger fellow-workers of the soil
> To wear for amulets. So others shall
> Take patience, labor, to their heart and hand
> From thy hand, and thy heart, and thy brave cheer,
> And God's grace fructify through thee to all.
> The least flower with a brimming cup may stand,
> And share its dew-drop with another near.

It is not true to say that we would all be heroic if our trials were on a great scale. The Divine Master said that only he who was faithful in the little things would be put over the great things. Heroism in the least is the pledge of heroism in the greatest. Unless we can bear up under the trifling trials, we go down under the great ones. When the small heartaches of the day are dignified by the thought of a Divine Purpose in them, then when the great trials come, they will have the Divine Image stamped on them.

Moses had to be told why Heaven so favored him, and the answer came that the Lord did not set His Love upon him because his people were more numerous than any other people of the world, for they were among the fewest, but because "the Lord loved you."

A man will often give reasons why he loves a woman; a woman will never give a reason why she loves. She rather imitates the Divine, saying: "Just because." This was the way God loved Moses and his people. This is the way, too, the little things of life are divinized and lifted in value above the stars—they are performed just because one loves God.

COURTESY

A GENERAL COMPLAINT heard by those who have lived through thirty or forty years of our times is the gradual disappearance of courtesy, politeness, and gentleness among men. There is no point in writing a lamentation about it; it is better to recall its true nature.

Courtesy is often regarded as a mere secular virtue due to gentle birth, high breeding, or affected social training. Its roots, however, are much deeper. As Hilaire Belloc wrote:

> *Of Courtesy, it is much less*
> *Than Courage of Heart or Holiness,*
> *Yet in my walks it seems to me*
> *That the Grace of God is in Courtesy.*

It is interesting that the only two men, outside of Our Blessed Lord, whom Scripture describes as "good men" were two men who practiced courtesy: Joseph of Arimathea and Barnabas. One manifested courtesy to the dead; the other to the living. The first braved the scorn of Roman politicians and the jeerings of a mob to beg for the Body of the Crucified Lord. Wrapping it in fine linen, he buried it in a tomb which he had reserved for himself, and which he probably used later on—for the Lord needed it only three days.

Barnabas, the other good man, was a sympathizer, a kindly soul who saw possibilities in others who were ignored or repugned. It was Barnabas who told the Apostles of the possibilities of Paul and finally enlisted him into their ranks. Both Joseph and Barnabas were rich men, but both of them were kind men.

The Divine Injunction: "Do to other men all that you would have them do to you" is not something negative in its encouragement of courtesy. It does not mean not leaving cigarette butts on the upholstery of Aunt Elsie's sofa because she may come and leave cigarette butts on your dining room chair. Rather, it is positive; namely, the doing of things to others such as you would like others to do to you. You would like them to remember you on your birthday, to write a note to you in your bereavement. It is a going out of the way to do nice things for people whether they be nice or not.

Courtesy and good manners are the crowning beauty of consecrated conduct; it is seeing the worth in others, because they are God's creatures and because in their own souls they may be a thousand times more worthy of His blessing. Everyone in the world carries around with him a certain moral atmosphere, which to a great extent determines his relations to fellow creatures. A beautiful woman who becomes insanely jealous of another beautiful woman and insults her has about her that fetid air of egotism which diffuses itself in the bad smell of discourtesy. Courtesy in its roots is saintliness; that is why sometimes one will find it in the most unlettered and uneducated, such as in the simple peasants in Europe; in such cases, there is often a gentleness which far surpasses the effete and superficial manners of the educated.

Goethe was right when he said, "There is no outward sign

of courtesy that does not rest on a deep moral foundation." Courtesy is love in action; not the love that seeks to be loved in return, but the love that puts affection in others, and finds them lovable.

SYMPATHY

ONE WONDERS if there is not more sympathy in smaller communities than in great cities. One can live in apartments and not know the next-door neighbor, but there is hardly a village in which one does not know the next-door neighbor. There is probably less borrowing of sugar in all of the apartments of New York City than there is in a village of five hundred. Not long ago, a picture magazine took photographs for one hour of people who passed by a wounded man on a subway stairs. The magazine recounted in pictures the number who looked at the man, and then went on their way without making a sympathetic inquiry. But the magazine itself forgot to state that the photographer was more interested in the click of his machine than he was in the tick of the heart of the wounded man.

This does not mean that sympathy is nonexistent, for the generous heart of Americans pours itself out in alms and in sympathy to the needy and the poor.

Sympathy is a temper or characteristic which draws others together. It is what might be called "conductivity." The Greek origin of the word "sympathy" implies "suffering with." It is a kind of silent understanding when heart meets heart. It is a form of substitution in which one takes the heart out of his own body and places it in the body of another man, and in exchange, takes back the other's heart. It is not mere pity, for pity can be like the traveler in the Gospel who looked on the wounded man, but did not help. Sentimentality can exist in low souls, but pure sympathy resides only in the noble.

Sometimes sympathy can be silent, particularly where there is grief. Saint Paul told the Romans: "Mourn with the mourner." The shedding of a common tear is far more eloquent than are honeyed words. This is well proven in the case of Job, whose comforters sat silently seven days beside him; their consolation was far greater than when they broke their silence and gave so many false reasons as to why Job suffered.

The foundation of all true sympathy and that which makes it universal, is love. The best of men can offer only human tenderness without understanding the mystery of pain and tears. But when one comes to the Love of Christ, one finds both the tenderness of the human and the comprehensiveness of the Divine. In Him alone is united sympathy and the understanding of the mystery of pain. It was that that made Him weep over the death of His beloved friend Lazarus. Many men have a heart, but they lack the mind to embrace the mystery. On the one hand, there can be narrow good men, and on the other hand, iron-hearted philanthropists; but in Christ, the tender heart and the Divine Knowledge combine and complete one another.

Hence, He bade us to have sympathy with all men, not in the way of condescension, not as the pure lifting their skirts from the impure; but as men touching to heal, as men hating the sin and loving the sinner. This sympathy alone can rid us of that modern pity which G. K. Chesterton so well condemns: "The practical weakness of the vast mass of modern pity for the poor and the oppressed is precisely that it is merely pity; but pity is pitiful, but not respectful. Men feel that the cruelty to the poor is a kind of cruelty to animals. They never feel it is injustice to equals, nay, it is treachery to comrades. This dark, scientific pity, this brutal pity, has an elemental sincerity of its own, but it is entirely useless for all ends of social reform."

When traveling in many Oriental countries, one may stop at the house of anyone and ask for hospitality. It will be extended not only for the night, but even for a longer period.

Love and Society

The natural sense of sympathy is deeper there than in our complex civilization where even giving a hitch-hiker a "lift" is forbidden. Too many abused the privilege and made sympathy unsafe.

Christian sympathy extends to those who are unsympathetic. A legend tells us that Abraham received a visitor in his tent. Abraham killed his best lamb, gave him his best cot, and served him as a servant. But the visitor was displeased with everything. After three days, Abraham put him out. The Lord appeared to Abraham saying: "Abraham, if I put up with him for forty years, can you not put up with him for three days?"

What has happened to that double side of sympathy which is the basis of the Christian philosophy of life: "Rejoice with those who rejoice, mourn with the mourner." It has been said that the wounded deer sheds tears, but it belongs only to man to weep with those who weep and, by sympathy, to divide another's sorrows and double another's joys.

In a nation, bad blood arises immediately when others are indifferent to our misfortunes. Nothing so spoils a people as a spirit which makes each say: "I am I and you are you, and that's the end of it." Rather, as the poet has said:

> *We, are we not formed as notes of music are*
> *For one another though dissimilar?*

Of the two kinds of sympathy, it seems easier to show sympathy with people in trouble than to rejoice with happy folk. In Shakespeare's *As You Like It*, there is a description of two brothers, each in love with his chosen mistress. One succeeds in his courtship, whereupon the other exclaims: "How bitter a thing it is to look into happiness through another man's eyes."

Furthermore, it seems to be easier to do one of these than to do both together. Some are more sensitive to pain in others, and others are more sensitive to joy in others. It could be that feeling the need of sympathy ourselves, we play a sympathetic tune on the keyboard of another; but why, it might be asked, since we all wish joy, why not share in another's joy?

It has been said that it becomes easier to do both as we grow older. One of the heroes of Homer sang:

> *Taught by time, my heart has learned to glow*
> *For others' good and weep at others' woe.*

Every man rejoices twice when he has a partner in his joy. He who shares tears with us wipes them away. He divides them in two, and he who laughs with us makes the joy double. Two torches do not divide, but increase the flame. Tears are more quickly dried up when they run on a friend's cheek in furrows of compassion.

How beautifully both these sympathies were revealed in the character of Our Blessed Lord when He saw the leper, the widow of Naim, the blind man by the wayside, the hungry multitudes distressed "as sheep without a shepherd." He touched the leper; He dried the tears of the widow; He was hungry with the hungry and he fed them. He suffered with their suffering. One day a publican made a great feast in his house. Our Lord sat down with His Disciples, saying that while the Bridegroom was with them, they should all rejoice. He also entered sympathetically into the joys of the marriage feast of Cana, even making better wine when the poor wine had been drained.

Few there are who can carry this sympathy to a point of forgiveness as Our Lord did from the Cross; as Saint Thomas More, Chancellor of England, did, for he gave a blessing to the persecutors. Just before being killed, he was asked if he had anything to say. His answer was:

> More have I not to say, my Lords, but that like as the blessed apostle St. Paul, as we read in the Acts of the Apostles, was present, and consented to the death of St. Stephen, and kept their clothes that stoned him to death, and yet be they now both twain holy saints in Heaven, and shall continue there friends forever, so I verily trust, and shall therefore right heartily pray, that though your Lordships have now here in earth been judges to my condemnation, we may yet here-

after in Heaven merrily all meet together, to our everlasting salvation. And thus I desire Almighty God preserve and defend the King's Majesty and to send him good counsel.

IDENTIFICATION

How OFTEN in helping others do we remain outside of their needs and pains, rarely identifying ourselves with them. One feels this particularly in visiting a leper colony where one mingles with, and touches, the victims of this disease. But after a few brief hours one leaves, only to feel the contrast with those who stay and who spend their lives among open wounds.

This want of identification is also experienced by the honest-minded social workers who relieve the want of others with other people's money, who spend the eight hours of working time in broken homes and with unfed children, and then leave them to their need, as one might leave a factory when the whistle blew.

Many there are in the world who personally bear the burden of others. They are missionaries. What a contrast between foreign aid and missionary aid! Foreign aid brings things, such as tractors, money, drills; missionaries bring themselves. Foreign aid bears the financial burden of assisting others; missionaries bear the persons on their backs. The ambassador of foreign aid has an avocation; the missionary has a vocation, or a life's work. Foreign aid relieves poverty; the missonary helps the poor. Foreign aid attacks the problem of ignorance; the missionary struggles with this ignorant boy or dull girl. When the job is finished, the representative of foreign aid leaves the distressed area; the missionary stays. The former lives in a hotel; the missionary shares the lot of those whom he serves.

Bringing this question of identification to the social order, one finds it strikingly expressed by Denis de Rougemont: "If my neighbor is stronger than I, I fear him; if he is weaker, I despise him; if we are equal, I resort to subterfuge. What motive could I have for obeying him, what reason for loving him?" How true. The help we give others is so often condescension. We look upon them as being in need, we being the suppliers. Heaven may look upon them, however, in a different way. It may be we who are in need, not the hungry and the naked. They only need food and drink, clothing and shelter. But we need to be tumbled from our jittery throne of superiority which rests upon such a fragile base as *having*.

On the other hand, how often when we are weaker than others, we abhor their strength, we envy their wealth, we regard their possessions as something having been filched from us. If they are learned, we call them snobs; if holy, we abominate them as hypocrites. The luxury and the wealth into which Soviet leaders have cast themselves is a proof that, in the long run, every Communist is nothing but a Capitalist without any cash in his pocket.

The world has in it countless examples of those who put on, not the cloak of the poor man, but rather his poverty. But whence comes the inspiration for this humbling of the seemingly superior self in order to become one with the needy? The question reaches its acute form in a nun in a leper colony. A visitor said to her as she was washing the feet of a leper: "I wouldn't do that for a million dollars!" "Neither would I," she answered. She did it because Our Blessed Lord, Who looked not upon His Divine Glory and His equality with the Father, but rather looked upon the helplessness and the danger and need of a Saviour of men. The lesson of all humiliation for the sake of others comes from God humbling Himself, and taking upon Himself the form of a man, not just merely helping him in the effects of sin, but in removing sin itself. He crossed a line into that area where afflicted humanity lives and never came back until He relieved the cause of that affliction. This is the foundation of all identification with the poor and the needy.

Just as hatred separates man from man, so love produces the harmony of feeling and interest that leads to the unity of service, and when this love is Divine, then man has an inspiration for doing more than throwing scraps of food to the needy. He throws even himself.

JUDGMENT

IN THE MIDST of all the talk of "cold wars," "co-existence," political alliances and international discord, no one ever seems to look at the world from the point of view of crisis or judgment, for crisis means judgment.

Judgment is everywhere in nature. If one does not eat, one gets a headache; if a farmer does not plant seed, he gets no harvest; what he sows, that also he reaps. God does not send a headache or scurvy to a man who does not eat; but He has made the universe in such a way that the failure to live according to His biological laws produces certain harmful effects. These effects are called judgments. So in the moral order, evil thoughts lead to evil actions. As Ralph Barton wrote some years ago about the judgment on his own life:

> I have had an exceptionally glamorous life, as life goes, and more than my share of appreciation and affection. . . . I have run from wife to wife, from house to house and from country to country in a ridiculous effort to escape from myself. In so doing, I am very much afraid that I have brought a great deal of unhappiness to those who have loved me. No one thing is responsible for this suicide and no one person—except myself.

What is true of nature and of persons is true of nations. Arnold Toynbee in his ten-volume *Study of History* has enumerated twenty-one civilizations of which we have historical records; only seven of them remain. He shows that the breakdown of civilization did not come from external causes, nor from the loss of command over environment, but from an inner decay and loss of the moral sense. Not even the increasing command over natural resources is found to be a condition of peace and happiness for a nation. "The increasing command over the environment," he writes, "in a disintegrating society, only serves in the end, to put a greater working power into the suicidally demented society's chosen work of self-destruction; and the story turns out to be a simple illustration of the thesis 'the wages of sin is death.'"

Egypt built its greatest pyramids on the eve of its decline. The great Russian writers of the nineteenth century have shown that in the twentieth century, society would develop in the way of increasing political and economic order with a spiritual and moral disorder. As the world becomes more unified commercially and politically, it could also become more chaotic and perverse in the hearts of its citizens.

What superficial minds are apt to miss is that outer unity of peoples is concomitant with inner discord. It could very well be that our danger is not from an outer barbarism, but from an inner barbarism; not from an attack from the outside, but from a moral rottenness from within. This inner suicide is not apparent to the masses; only a few diagnosticians can see it. The masses miss it because they fall in with the tendency to reject anything and everything that suggests "badness," "evil," "sin," or "guilt." The latest move in this direction from the sinners who deny their sin is to protest against saying that bad boys and bad girls are "juvenile delinquents." There is no longer a target that is missed, a law that is disobeyed, a love that is rejected, a God who is blasphemed.

All this is a rehearsal for crisis. And crisis is Judgment, and Judgment is God allowing a God-forsaking world to reap the Dead Sea apples it planted.

TRUE GIVING

LOVE HAS nothing to do with usefulness. There would be no love if a person kept a list of index cards on which were noted the so-called friends who might be helpful to him. Neither does love cultivate a friend because "he can get it for me wholesale"; love does not cherish another person because of the pleasure that person gives; love does not give money in great abundance to a political party in order to become a foreign ambassador; love does not give gifts to prostitute. Love, in a word, has nothing to do with calculation.

One day when Our Blessed Lord was at dinner in the little village of Bethany, just a short time before His Passion and Death, a woman stole into the dining room and broke a vessel of precious ointment, pouring it over His feet. Judas, who was present at the dinner, immediately asked: "Why all this waste? It might have been sold." On the part of the penitent woman who loved, there was no calculation of cost; on the part of the disciple who had lost his faith, there was the reckoning of profit. Her love knew no limits, but his seeming interest was made up of that which Wordsworth said Heaven spurns: "Heaven rejects the lore of nicely calculated less or more."

Judas never saw the woman with repentance in her heart, for he was asked by the Master if he had really seen her. The fact that he priced the gift in terms of money proved that he never understood its meaning, for if he had, he would have known that it was priceless. Judas was one who knew the price of everything, and the value of nothing. Within a few days he would put the price of thirty pieces of silver upon his Lord. He might have seen the perfume, but there was something more than perfume in that scene.

Priceless things cannot be bought. The Lord could not be bought, but He could be sold. One can buy a book of poetry, but one cannot buy poetry. The understanding of it is something far beyond the price of the book. As Lowell put it:

> At the devil's booth are all things sold,
> Each ounce of dross costs its ounce of gold;
> For a cap and bells our lives we pay,
> Bubbles we buy with a whole soul's tasking:
> 'Tis Heaven alone that is given away,
> 'Tis only God may be had for the asking;
> No price is set on the lavish summer;
> June may be had by the poorest comer.

Love never needs any justification. Men will very often give reasons why they love, but a woman never gives a reason; she considers love its own justification. The offerings of love are never wasted. Flowers are sent to the bedridden when something perhaps more useful might have been sent. But the flowers are the offerings of love and as such are accepted. The value of a gift is not in what was paid for it, but the sacrifice and devotion of the giver. That is why we tear off price tags when we give gifts, in order to prove that there is no correspondence between the gift of the lover and the love of the giver. But is it not true that love is more often stronger when it descends than when it ascends? Mothers love children more than children love parents. And God loves us more than we love Him. We measure out our love to Him drop by drop; He breaks the alabaster vase of His Body and gives His all for our redemption.

Love and Marriage

CASTLES IN SPAIN

You CAN imagine a mountain of gold. Do you think that you will ever see one? You can imagine a castle with a thousand rooms, some you see with walls of diamonds, emeralds, amethysts, and star sapphires. But do you think you will ever see such a castle?

The imagination, because it is a power of the soul, can imagine the infinite. But reality is finite, cabined, cribbed, confined, and limited. Hence arises the disproportion between what we imagined something to be, and what it turns out to be in the concrete.

Because one imagines oneself perfectly happy in love with another, it does not follow that it will always be so. Every man promises every woman something that only God alone can give—perfect contentment, perfect joy. Every woman promises every man something that only God can give—perfect love, perfect happiness. In order to avoid the test of reality, all films and romantic novels about love end with the classic expression: "And they lived happily ever after." They make it appear that marriage is a conclusion, when really it is a point of departure.

The woman later on discovers that the man will never be able to find anything in a closet or a dresser. He will never say a word of thanks for the best prepared menu. He will throw his clothes in a heap on a chair, and then complain that the clothes were not pressed. He who formerly seemed to be a knight and a Prince Charming, because imagination crowned him with an aureole of perfection, is now just a man. Every woman marries a man and lives with a husband; every man marries a woman and lives with a wife.

But marriage is not a snare or an illusion because it does not fulfill all dreams. The reality, which very often young people refuse to see, can be just as beautiful as the dream —though it is vastly different from the dream. Many a husband or wife, years after marriage, says: "When I was married, I thought I loved my wife (or my husband) so much that it would be impossible to love more. Now I know that that sentiment was nothing compared to the love I have today."

An old friend came to visit a young married man and said to him: "I am an old friend of the family. I knew your wife before you married." The young man answered: "Unfortunately, I did not know her until I married her." Every bride is half woman and half dream; every groom is half man and half dream.

No present love can be insured for the future. Love is something that is tested by time. It grows not because of its intensity at the beginning. As a matter of fact, the intensity of passion at the beginning could be a sign that it would more quickly burn itself out. Love is strong, not because it is passionate, but because it has the power of self-renewal, that is, it will mount to higher and higher stages by acts of self-denial.

True love is not so much expression in desire to possess another, as it is in consideration for the other person who is loved. It may not mean so much to say: "Oh, how I love you," as to say: "Don't go out without your rubbers." A French novelist makes a character in his novel say that to his wife. They were astounded when a maiden aunt who lived with them for years, without any apparent discontent, suddenly burst into tears of weeping when she heard those words, and said: "No one ever cared whether or not I had my rubbers."

LOVE AND REALITY

LOVE AT the beginning is a paradise. Its foundation is a dream that each one has found to be something unique and a happiness which is eternal. That is why all love songs of the theater sing of "how happy we shall be." Love songs treat what is in prospect, not what is in retrospect. This is because there is a kind of infinity about imagining what will happen, while there is only reality about what has already happened. The young still dream dreams of the future; the old, like Horace, look back to the "glorious past." This is not in any way to minimize the value of paradisal future, but merely to place love in its ontological setting. Every great thing begins with a dream, whether it be that of the engineer who plans a bridge, or of the heart that plans a home. The soul draws upon its infinity and colors it with the gold of paradise. No one ever climbs to the heavens without passing through the clouds, and at the beginning every lover has his head in the clouds.

This foretaste of Heaven is good, and even Heaven-sent. It is the advance agent of Heaven, telling the heart of that real happiness which lies ahead. Actually, it is a bait, a blueprint, a John the Baptist, an announcer telling of the program yet to come. If God did not permit this preview of joy, who would venture in beyond the vestibule?

Love does not continue with the same ecstasy. Because flesh is the medium of married love, it suffers the penalty of the flesh; it becomes used to affection. As life goes on, a greater stimulus is required to produce an equal reaction to sensation. The eye can soon become used to beauty, and the fingers to the touch of a friend. The intimacy which at first was so desirable, now becomes at times a burden. The "I-want-to-be-alone feeling," and the "I-think-I-will-go-home-to-mother feeling" strip the eye of its rose-colored glasses. Bills coming into the kitchen make love fly out of the parlor. The very habit of love becomes boring, because it is a habit and not an adventure. Perhaps the yearning for a new partner accompanies a disgust with the old partner. The care of children, with their multiplying accidents and diseases, tends to bring love down from its vision in the clouds to periodical, realistic visitations to the nursery.

Sooner or later those living the affective life are brought face to face with this problem: Is love a snare and a delusion? Does it promise what it cannot give? No, life is not a mockery. One has not hit the bottom of life, but only the bottom of one's ego. One has not hit the bottom of his soul, but only of his instinct; not the bottom of his mind, but of his passions; not the bottom of his spirit, but of his sex. The aforementioned trials are merely so many contacts with reality which Almighty God sends into every life, for what we are describing here is common to every life. If life went on as a dream without the shock of disillusionment, who would ever attain his final goal with God and perfect happiness? The majority of men would rest in mediocrity; acorns would be content to be saplings; some children would never grow up and nothing would mature.

Therefore, God had to keep something back, namely, Himself in eternity; otherwise we would never push forward. So He makes everyone run up against a stone wall every now and then in life; on such occasions they feel the crisis of nonentity and have an overwhelming sense of nothingness and loneliness, in order that they may see life not as a city but as a bridge to eternity. The dryness in human love is not dry rot; it should be the dryness that ripens to the love of God.

MODERN WOMAN

MODERN WOMAN has been made equal with man, but she has not been made happy. She has been "emancipated," like a pendulum removed from a clock and now no longer free to swing, or like a flower which has been emancipated from its roots. She has been cheapened in her search for mathematical equality in two ways: by becoming a victim of man and a victim of the machine. She became a victim of man by becoming only the instrument of his pleasure and ministering to his needs in a sterile exchange of egotisms. She became a victim of the machine by subordinating the creative principle of life to the production of non-living things, which is the essence of Communism.

This is not a condemnation of a professional woman, because the important question is not whether a woman finds favor in the eyes of a man, but whether she can satisfy the basic instincts of womanhood. The problem of a woman is whether certain God-given qualities, which are specifically hers, are given adequate and full expression. These qualities are principally devotion, sacrifice, and love. They need not necessarily be expressed in a family, nor even in a convent. They can find an outlet in the social world, in the care of the sick, the poor, the ignorant; in the seven corporal works of mercy. It is sometimes said that the professional woman is hard. This may, in a few instances, be true, but if so, it is not because she is in a profession, but because she has alienated her profession from contact with human beings in a way to satisfy the deeper cravings of her heart. It may very well be that the revolt against morality and the exaltation of sensuous pleasure as the purpose of life are due to the loss of the spiritual fulfillment of existence. Having been frustrated and disillusioned, such souls first become bored, then cynical, and finally, suicidal.

The solution lies in a return to the Christian concept, wherein stress is placed not on equality, but on equity. Equality is law. It is mathematical, abstract, universal, indifferent to conditions, circumstances, and differences. Equity is love, mercy, understanding, and sympathy. It allows the consideration of details, appeals, and even departures from fixed rules which the law has not yet embraced. In particular, it is the application of law to an individual person. Equity places its reliance on moral principles and is guided by an understanding of the motives of individual families which fall outside the scope of the rigors of law.

Equity, therefore, rather than equality should be the basis of all the feminine claims. Equity is the perfection of equality, not its substitute. It has the advantage of recognizing the specific difference between man and woman, which equality does not have. Man and woman are equal inasmuch as they have the same rights and liberties, the same final goal of life, and the same redemption by the blood of Our Saviour; but they are different in function. It is because man and woman are unequal that they complement one another.

When man loves woman, it follows that the nobler the woman, the nobler the love, and the higher the demands made by a woman, the more worthy a man must be. That is why woman is the measure of the level of our civilization. It is for our age to decide whether woman shall claim equality in sex and the right to work with men, or whether she will claim equity and give to the world that which no man can give. In pagan days, when women want only to be equal with men, they have lost respect. In Christian days, when men were strongest, woman was most respected. The choice before women in this day of the collapse of justice is whether to equate themselves with men in rigid exactness, or to rally to equity, mercy, and love, giving to a lawless world something that equality can never give.

THE PROGRESSION OF LOVE

THE ONLY really progressive thing in all the universe is love. And yet that which God made to bloom and blossom and flower through time and into eternity is that which is most often nipped in the bud. Perhaps that is the reason why artists always picture love as a little Cupid who never grows up. Armed with only a bow and arrow in an atomic universe, the poor little angel has hardly a chance. Saint Paul speaks of faith and hope disappearing in heaven, but love remaining forever. Yet the one thing that mortals want to be eternal is that which they most quickly choke before it has begun to walk. If a man came from Mars and had never heard of the greatest event in history, which was the birth of the Divine Love in the person of Christ, he probably could guess the rest of the story and predict His Crucifixion. All he would need to do would be to look at the way even the best of human loves are divorced, denied, mutilated, bartered, and stunted.

But if love be what the heart wants above all things else, why does it not grow in love? It is because most hearts want love like a serpent, not like a bird. They want love on the same plane as the flesh, and not a love which wings its way from earth to mountain peak and then is lost in the sky. They want a love that, like Cupid, does not grow; not a love which dies in order to ascend, like the Risen Christ, who accepts defeat and conquers it by Love. They want the impossible: repetition without satiety, which no human body can give. The refusal to surrender the horizontal for the vertical, because it demands sacrifice, condemns the heart to mediocrity and staleness. Love is no bargain. It appears so attractive, like a precious violin advertised at a low price, but one discovers that after one has it without much effort it is useless unless one disciplines himself to its use. The cross is a far better picture of what love really is than Cupid. The latter's darts are shot in the dark in a moment when the heart least suspects it; but the cross is something one sees on the roadway of life a long time ahead, and the invitation to carry it to a resurrection of love is frightening indeed. That is why the Lord has so few lovers. They want that cross streamlined, without Him who said: "If any man has a mind to come My way, let him renounce self, and take up his cross daily, and follow Me."

Few have described sacrificial love in marriage better than Antoine-Frédéric Ozanam in his *History of Civilization in the Fifth Century:*

> Marriage is something greater than a contract, for it involves also a sacrifice. The woman sacrifices an irreparable gift, which was the gift of God and was the object of her mother's anxious care: her fresh young beauty, frequently her health, and that faculty of loving which women have but once. The man, in his turn, sacrifices the liberty of his youth, those incomparable years which never return; the power of devoting himself to her whom he loves, which is vigorous only in his early years; and the ambition—inspired by love—to create a happy and glorious future. All this is possible but once in a man's life—perhaps never. Therefore Christian marriage is a double oblation, offered in two chalices, one filled with virtue, purity and innocence; the other with unblemished self-devotion, the immortal consecration of a man to her who is weaker than himself, who was unknown to him yesterday, and with whom today he is content to spend the remainder of his life. These two cups must be both filled to the brim in order that the union may be holy and Heaven may bless it.

EVOLUTION

Love is an evolution, a growth, and a pilgrimage. The first stage is the act of choice, with its tremendous joy of discovery, the meeting of one's soul with another. This choice is made in enthusiasm. It implies an exclusive renouncement of the life that has gone before, and the release from anything that would restrain. It implies a detachment of all that is not pleasing to the other. Even renouncements of other allurements, because they are done in love and enthusiasm, are never considered difficult. With this choice there comes the desire of union and the urge to know one better, to understand and be understood, the need of being loved, the desire of security, the search for the repose of the heart which will be the perfection of one's being.

The second stage is union. It is the afternoon of love. It is the taking possession of one another in a reciprocal gift. Each one gives self to the other in a double movement of gift and welcome, where the joy of giving is sweetly defeated by the thrill of being received.

This is a moment of the sensible Presence of God, and one that Saint Thomas compares to the Ascension. It is an ecstasy like a ray from the sun, which is God.

The real definition of love is that it is a mutual self-giving which ends in self-recovery. If love were only a mutual self-giving, it would end in exhaustion. But there ultimately comes a moment where there is a self-recovery, and the beginning of the family. Even where there is no child, love begins to interiorize. There is a stage reached where it is no longer the body that leads the soul; it is the soul that leads the body. Through a loving war of little acts of self-denial, a couple finally take possession of that citadel which is not won by passion, but by an application of the Cross of Christ for love of one another—and from the fastness of that castle, few there are who seek to stray.

There is now no longer a forced unison, but discovered harmony. There comes now a larger learning, not at the cost of tears, but a service and dedication to the other. The glamour passes. They are no longer two instruments, toneless with self-love and overstrung with pride; love now plays with patient fingers on the string that produced harmony for the children of God.

Returning to the child as the fruit of their love, it is seen how closely related it is to the Birth of Christ. All love ends in an incarnation, or a taking on of flesh, even as God took on flesh in the Incarnation.

The couple see themselves as a quarry from which God is hewing every soul they bring into the world as an eligible stone, capable of being squared and shaped for service, however slowly, in the heavenly Temple of God. The husband and wife who become father and mother now see themselves as summoned to be the architects with God of that spiritual house which is built of living stones. The child upon whom they look is the fruit of prayerful love, and not of unsanctified desire.

The husband and wife see that their lives would be frustrated if, like an imbecile farmer, they planted His seed in the earth and then tore it up, or planted the vine and then uprooted it, or touched the bow to the violin, and never made a melody, or a chisel to marble and never produced a statue.

THE CRESCENDO OF LOVE

As stated in the last article, love is a mutual self-giving which ends with self-recovery and the beginning of a family.

Love, which deliberately frustrates self-recovery, could produce dual selfishness. It could be likened to a perpetual change in barter, like commerce between two shipwrecked sailors on a desert isle, yielding no profit to others or to themselves, and with no other destiny but to be consumed in the useless fire their own hearts had kindled. Love is a loan from the Heart of God, and must not be buried in a napkin. It must be paid back again to Him in fruit, in a fulfillment of the marriage.

The child who is born now gives concrete expression to that love they always spoke of as "ours." Lovers always imply that the love that binds them together is something more than the sum or addition of one and one making two. Implied is the idea that there is some bond outside of them, stronger than either, uniting them both. As the Holy Spirit is the great bond of love between father and son, the child now becomes "our love" in the flesh.

In the mother, particularly, redemption vests itself because she becomes the sacristan and the guardian, the trustee and the wardess of their love. No longer is she the instrument for satisfying a passing fascination, a banquet to be consumed and forgotten; but rather, his lifemate, the increaser and the multiplier of their image, of their virtues and their grace.

Here in the child is found the challenge to death. For their survival in new life is the conquest of death and the pledge of their own immortality. Like the burning bush that Moses saw, their love burns but is not consumed, for it produces the vision of a new creature of God.

The modern age, which is so keen on enthroning sex, may not be far from the truth when they say: "Love is God," for if they would enter a little further into the mystery, they would see that what they must learn is that God is Love. This is true not only because their love is an incarnation, such as Christ in the cradle or the stable, but it is also a Saviour as Christ on Calvary, for the child is the redeemer or the savior of their love from death.

Love summoned them first to be creators in the broad sense that they create their love, thanks to God's power.

Thus there is a gradual crescendo of love. First, almost with childish minds, they say that God does not forbid them to love. Then they understand a little later on that God, being love, has united them one to another, and has placed in them a great hope for continuing His creation. Then they discover successively the joy of loving one another for God, then of loving God in the other, and then of loving the other with the very love of God Himself. Their love then becomes a kind of an Advent, preparing for the coming of the Messiah or Christ. It is a temporal mission with great eternal consequences.

The weakness of human affections never suffices for a lasting love. They are but two empty vessels, and each of them must be filled with the wine of God.

Love and Children

WHAT CHILDREN ARE LIKE

No "OLD" people ever enter the Kingdom of Heaven. We have Divine warrant for this statement, though it was not put exactly in these words. When the Son of God came to this earth He said: "The man who does not welcome the Kingdom of God like a child, will never enter into it." He did not mean that we had to be childish, but we had to be childlike. What are the qualities of the child which are so essential for an adult acquiring the eternal youthfulness of Heaven?

The first characteristic of a child is that he bathes in the infinite and the eternal. The present is thought by him to be enduring. He cannot understand the past; therefore, death is beyond his comprehension. He cannot understand what is yet to be, or things otherwise than they actually are. Impermanence escapes the child completely. Perhaps one of the reasons why a child feels so sorrowful when the mother leaves the house is because he eternalizes her absence. It has been said that dogs have exactly the same sense of total loss when the master leaves them.

The child is a voyager without any baggage. He lives in the present and imagines it to be eternal. He can mount a broomstick and imagine himself to be the king of infinite space. No doll is a rag to a little girl; it is flesh and blood. Beanstalks actually climb to the heavens. It is only as the years pass on, and with them the sense of eternity, that the child becomes impressed with transition, which underlies all creation. From a psychological point of view, therefore, the smaller becomes the world as we grow older. As an adult loses his sense of eternity, he becomes caught in a kind of whirlpool in which his ego is drawn closer and closer into himself until he finally is imprisoned in his own selfishness.

The second characteristic of the child is innocence. The child hardly perceives disorder or evil, or at least does not remark upon them as such. Whatever exists for the child is good and also true. The innocence of the child is directly related to the religious sentiment which has its starting point in filial sentiment or love for the parents. Until the age of six, there is an admiration for the parents which is without limit. He attributes to them omniscience, power, goodness, and truth. He cannot imagine any father in the world being stronger than his father, nor any mother being better than his mother. It is not difficult later on to translate these attributes into their source, which is God Himself.

There is a tremendous receptivity for the truths of religion, though at this age it is not necessary to give the reason for these truths. The teaching of religion is very much like the teaching of cleanliness to children. We teach them the habits of cleanliness, and then only later on do they learn hygiene and the reasons for cleanliness. So too, we teach them the Truth and the Goodness of God, and only later on do they learn the reason for the submission and their love.

If it be objected that there is hate in children, it must be stated that children only hate when they are hated. A child is teased by his older brother, which causes him to react with a similar feeling. Children hated by their parents grow up in hate. Where there is no environment and atmosphere of love, hate multiplies as it does in the crowded subway. The arctic regions would have as many oranges as California, if they had as much sun. So children that grow up in an atmosphere of love become sweet-tempered and kind. It is very difficult to convince children to love God, unless they first have been loved and know the experience of it. Francis Thompson, catching the full spirit of the innocence of the child, said: "Look for me in the nurseries of Heaven."

GUILT

A surplus of affection toward children is very often the result not of a true love but of a defective authority. It does not take a child long to discover that he can get anything from his parents. Such false kindness makes the child more rebellious because he knows by experience that the commands of the mother are not sustained by a firm will. Furthermore, the child knows his own revolt will finally make the affectionate mother give way.

Some parents believe that the child ought not to submit to rule either in school or family. The greatest crime that one can commit against a child, according to this theory, is to refuse to leave the child in peace. Commands, it is said, will develop in him a guilt complex.

This doctrine ruins the very value which it sought, to preserve the liberty of the child. Self-government is confused with license. The child by definition is a weak creature, and has need of educative support to deliver him from weakness which is normal in his evolution. The false concept of liberty inferiorizes the child, creates a perpetual temptation to anarchy, which the child becomes unable to resist.

True parental authority is a moral force which is characterized by firmness wedded to gentleness. In virtue of the moral and intellectual superiority, the parent supplies the deficiencies of the child, his ignorance, and his need of guidance.

This moral superiority will be characterized by decision. All indecision is a mark of an inferior or one who is not able to guide. But there will also be gentleness, because one is in possession of true power. Severity is not to be confounded with authoritarianism. Authoritarianism is often due to a want of patience, but severity does not act out of sudden feeling.

Moral force is like running water in a narrow channel. It rushes forward to the field where it is to dispense fertility, but it must have barriers to confine its energies and direct its course. The difference between a swamp and a river is that the swamp has no bank. The parent who is guided by emotions is a swamp, without limits or control.

As the parents surrender authority, the state begins to take it over. Bad children become bad citizens. Disorder in the house becomes disorder in the nation. The state today is gradually taking over, in delinquents, that area of responsibility which properly belongs to parents, but which they have surrendered by refusing to exercise God-given control.

Honor is more than obedience. Honor is grounded upon the moral dignity of the parents. The parent must be vigilant over the child in April lest the frost of May destroy his blossoms. While he is a tender twig, he can be straightened.

If the example of parents is contrary to moral virtue, disastrous consequences follow. Their authority will be vitiated because all true obedience is connected with affection, and reference must be secured by moral influence. The external form or command may remain, but the inner life which is inspired by morality is wanting.

To every child, parents are the mirrors of perfection: The father is the strongest, the mother is the nicest. The two images in some way confound and reveal the Sovereign Justice and the Merciful Goodness of God. Without this concept of the Justice and Mercy of God, the child may become sulky and aggressive and moody. With it, a love of his parents will deepen, and he will be prepared to become a parent one day, conscious that in the home he will train his child in the infinite eternal truth.

GUIDANCE

NEVER BEFORE WAS there so much education in the world, and never before so little coming to the knowledge of the truth. Never before so much wealth; never before so much poverty. Never before has there been so much power; never before has power been so used for the destruction of human life. What is lacking is not method, but a goal. This particularly applies to parents who lack a coherent body of convincing standards to offer their children for guidance. They have sextants, but they have no fixed stars. They are surrounded by techniques, but no knowledge of destiny. They have material with which to build, but no blueprints. The tragedy, perhaps, is not so much that parents have lost their souls, but rather that they doubt whether they have souls to save. The same applies to their children.

When a modern painting confronts us with a part of a face, a twisted limb divided by a broken wheel, surmounted by a geometrical figure in a bird cage from which a purple cow's head stares crazily across a shore to a woman's body upside down, we realize that we are glaring into the tragedy of our times—a broken personality, a ruined human nature, a false concept of man. How can parents give to children what they themselves lack? Rudyard Kipling once said: "Give me the first six years of a child's life, and you can take the rest." Napoleon was once asked: "When does the education of a child begin?" and his answer was: "Twenty years before its birth, in the education of its mother."

Parents seem to forget that children are to be trained, a law which applies even to the animal kingdom. It is to be noted that some animals are much more capable of training than others. An elephant can be trained, but not a flea; a dog can be trained, but not a fly. When one comes to children, what is forgotten is that if children are not trained by their parents, they will be trained in spite of their parents. There is no such thing as a parent deciding that he will leave the child's mind empty as regards religious and moral education. The child's mind cannot be kept empty; it will be filled with something. Passions alone make it impossible for the mind of a child to be in a state of perpetual vacancy.

All neglect of training of the child is degeneration. Nature itself sounds this warning. Naturalists tell us that moles once had eyes to see but, having chosen to grovel in the darkness away from the sun, they lost their capacity to see. The words of the Gospel seemed almost hurled at the mole, like a judgment: "Take the talent away."

A child is like an octopus. Its arms will reach out for something, whether that something be food or poison. Radio, television, alleys, servants, playgrounds, pictures, books—all are teachers. What goes into the mind can be just as poisonous as what can go into the body. A mother would not allow her child to eat from a garbage can, and yet when that garbage is translated into evil for the mind, there is no shirking from its reception.

The parent has a double duty to put the truths of the natural order into the child's mind, and also the truths about God and its final destiny. But there is a difference in the way that each is assimilated. Natural truths must be known in order to be loved, but divine truths must be loved in order to be fully known. One cannot love music unless he knows it, but the more one loves it the better it is understood. Where is this love of virtue to come from in the heart of the child if it be not already possessed by the parent? We love because we have been loved. An infant that does not find in his parents all the love that he ought to find is in some way impaired in his discovery of God. When the Apostles drove away the children, Our Lord rebuked them and was much displeased. In fact, the strongest word that could be found in Greek for "rebuke" is used in the Gospel on this occasion. It was used in only one other instance, and that was against the Apostles James and John for seeking first places. If, therefore, the Lord was angry with His own who drove the children away, then what shall be the anger of God against parents who have not allowed their children to come to Him?

CHILDREN AND OBEDIENCE

PERHAPS WE ARE too hard on children. They are blamed when the fault often times lies with the parent. No child is ever smart enough to know the reason for an attitude he may have toward his parents. Later on, he comes to discover it, and knows that he was right. For example, when I was a boy, my mother would often call me when I was playing either baseball or football. It seemed so unfair to me to have my game interrupted to go to the store to buy soap or meat. She would justify her actions by saying: "What difference does it make whether you run on the field or run to the store? You are running in both cases."

When I grew up, I began to read the most learned philosopher the world has ever known—Thomas Aquinas. He has a treatise on work and play. In it I found verified something that I was unable to explain to my mother, namely, "There is a difference between work and play." Thomas Aquinas explained it this way: Work has a purpose; play has no purpose. Life must also have moments when there is recreation and, he even adds, nonsense. Now I know that there is a world of difference between running the bases and running to the store, but then I was not old enough to know it.

Perhaps if we inquire into the rebellion of children against their parents, we may find that they have some instinctive feeling that the parents have no right to command them, but they cannot put their finger on it. Could it not be this: Where do their parents get the authority to command them? Do they recognize that authority? Do they ever appeal to it? Are they themselves breaking an entirely different set of rules, but which are far less sacred than the ones which we are breaking? Why is it that all of their directions to me begin with "don't"? (One psychologist counted the "don'ts" of a mother to a child in an afternoon, and they added up to 292.)

Is it more wrong for me to walk into the house with dirty feet than it is for my mother to leave my father and marry another man? Why cannot I have my third cookie, when my father always has his fifth cocktail? Has my father, who uses dirty language to my mother, the right to tell me not to eat with dirty hands?

No child ever explicitly asks these questions, but they are half buried in his unconscious mind. Later on he may find the answer to some of them, as I found the difference between work and play. There will come a time when he will stumble upon it; perhaps it will be a text in a scripture: "children obey your parents in the Lord, for that is right." Note that there is a limitation to obedience, namely "in the Lord." It is the parents' right to command, for they may say to the child: "I must have you obedient, for I am responsible to God for you doing so."

On the other hand, the child is encouraged to obey. "In obeying my parents, I am doing that which is pleasing to God, and I do it because the Lord so bids me." Children are to obey their parents as long as their commands agree with those of God, and no further. If they required their children to steal or lie or cheat, or do anything wrong, they would not be called upon to do so.

Many parents today go on the principle that every single desire the child has must be satisfied. In this way, they say they will preserve the love of their children. Children love them because of what they get, not because of what they are. When a child grows up, the admiration he has for his parents is based only on the nobility of their character, piety, love for one another, and not the fact that they bought him expensive playthings to prepare him to use the world as his plaything.

Parents who live in the Lord will never have a problem of obedience. Children are wiser than we think.

TEEN-AGERS

A TEEN-AGER is in the first of one of the three great crises of life; the other two crises are apt to come in middle age and in old age, and neither of them is as serious as the first, which is the crisis of youth.

The three crises have to do with the body as regards youth, the mind as regards middle age, and things as regards old age. Each of these three: the body, the mind, and possessions or things, are all good in themselves, but they are capable of being perverted, just as fire is good, but it becomes bad when it burns down the house. The division between these ages is not absolute and rigid, for there is apt to be an inordinate desire of flesh, power, or things in any age. But middle age is apt to be more concerned with pride, power, egotism, from which will flow jealousy, hate, and envy, and getting ahead by trampling on others. Old age very often seeks a substitute for immortality through avarice or greed, believing that one has worth because one is wealthy.

But our principal interest here is with the teen-ager. There is a rush of biological sap into the tree of life at the beginning of teen-age. This tremendous vital energy that flows into youth is popularly called "sex," though that is not a good name for it. This biological urge does not only affect the body, but also the mind. The repercussions in the body are easily recognized, such as desire for the opposite sex, the immediacy of carnal values, and a morbid curiosity about its meaning. But its effect on the mind is of even greater importance. In fact, there are two changes of life; one at the beginning of the reproductive powers, and the other at their end. The second receives much attention, but the first has an equal importance. It accounts for the giddiness, the unpredictability, the anti-social attitudes of teen-agers. Parents are not to become discouraged about this teen-age mentality; they will grow out of it sanely and helpfully, but only on condition that they are properly directed.

There are certain things a teen-ager must remember about this vital urge which seems to make so many demands:

1. It comes from God, who has put into every human being two tremendous urges in order to assure both individual and social life. In the individual life, He has implanted a hunger, or a love of eating, which assures personal life. In order to assure the propagation of the human species, Almighty God has implanted a pleasure associated with the social order. Both of these pleasures come from the Creator, and can become wrong when they are used in a disordered way.

2. The second point is that this vital urge is called sex, but the teen-ager must never believe that man is to be understood in terms of sex. It is sex that is to be understood in terms of man. An automobile is not to be understood in terms of a clutch; it is to be understood in terms of its entire mechanism. Sex in a human being is not the same as sex in an animal. It would, therefore, be quite wrong to say that everyone must follow his nature, because our nature is different from that of a pig. The human nature is rational; that is to say, it is governed by a conscience. Hence, the instinct, or the urge, or the vital push is to be understood in terms of right and wrong, and not merely in terms of desire.

The animal loves the pleasure; a human being loves a person. Sex is replaceable, but love is not. What happens, therefore, in a human being is quite different from what would happen in the animal order.

YOUTH AND MORALITY

The term "teen-agers" is not a particularly exact way to describe youth, because the span between thirteen and nineteen is too great. By seventeen, generally, most youths are made. A very well-known biographer of Napoleon stated that at fifteen "he was already formed; true, life had something to add to it, but all the defects and good qualities were there in his fifteenth year." Mussolini, fighting with his classmates when he was fifteen, had manifested the same characteristics that he manifested later on. He himself wrote: "I was then formed. I fear that the influences I underwent then were decisive."

What has happened before the fifteenth year is very much like the dripping of water on a winter day. If the water is clear, the icicle will be clear; if dirty, the icicle will be dirty. If one puts garbage into the stomachs of children, it will be easy to forecast their health; if moral garbage is put into the minds of children, it is easy to predict how these ideas will pass out into act.

Recently there was held a United Nations Congress on the prevention of crime. It is strange to say that no one spoke out more strongly against all pornographic, horror publications and immoral literature than did L. N. Smirnov of the Soviet Union. He dealt with those who contend that to restrain immoral literature is to curtail freedom, saying: "Talking about human rights in connection with putting this degrading matter before juveniles is like the devil quoting the Bible."

This does not mean that youth already bent in the direction of evil cannot become virtuous, for with the grace of God, nothing is impossible. But our present situation rather suggests that youth becomes acquainted with the knowledge of good and evil at too precocious an age. On the morning of an important battle, Napoleon took away from his tent a portrait of his son, the King of Rome. This portrait had been there for several days before the battle in order to inspire his men. As the bitter struggle was about to begin, he ordered it removed, saying: "It is too soon for him to see a battlefield."

Youth presently is handicapped inasmuch as the major direction of their lives is in the hands of sociologists and psychologists, neither of whom have in their scientific equipment what Dr. Alexis Carrel says are the two essential conditions for developing character: isolation and discipline. Both of these come under the domain of religion and morality. As long as the youth travel in herds with their eyes fixed on a one-octave banjo player, they are incapable of reconstructing themselves. As Dr. Carrel put it: "A mode of life which imposes on everyone a constant effort, a psychological and moral discipline and privation, is necessary. An ascetic and mystical minority would rapidly acquire an irresistible power over the self-indulgent and spineless majority." Then he goes on to say that without this moral self-denial, the intelligence itself becomes anemic. The problem then is not what to do with teen-agers; it is who will train them in the Ten Commandments and morality before they are sixteen and seventeen.

BEING THANKFUL

A VERY INTERESTING phenomenon in children is that gratitude or thankfulness comes relatively late in their young lives. They almost have to be taught it; if not, they are apt to grow up thinking that the world owes them a living. How often grown sons and daughters after marriage and after some years spent in caring for their children, will say: "I never knew before how much love my parents put into raising me." Thanksgiving Day comes late in the year, and thanksgiving comes late in life.

Saint Paul had to teach his people gratitude to God by reminding them: "What powers hast thou, that did not come to thee by gift? And if they came to thee by gift, why dost thou boast of them, as if there were no gift in question?" Some believe that one should not plant trees if their fruit cannot be eaten in one's lifetime. This forgetfulness that others planted trees for the present generation is a kind of childishness.

The point here is not that children are naturally ungrateful, but rather that there is another attitude which precedes it, and that is praise. Though their parents have to be constantly telling them when to: "Say 'thank you,'" they never have to tell them to be enthusiastic about something which pleases them. They ignite quickly at the prospect of a bicycle, candy, a picnic, or a toy. They run out and tell everyone in the block what they received. It may be a new dress the mother gave, or a new baseball glove the father gave, or a trip they will make with their grandmother. Nothing so much cools off their burning ardor as the failure of someone to react warmly to the great things that have befallen them.

But what is praise? It is made up of two factors: first, a knowledge about something good or pleasurable or happy; second, an emotional inability to keep still about it. Secrets are hard to keep, because they are about something not generally known, and therefore destined to cause an interesting recoil. In this, praise differs from thanksgiving, because it takes only two persons to have gratitude: the one who did the favor, and the one who received it. But it takes three to have praise: both of the above, and someone delighted by the favor bestowed.

In a society which is as individualistic as ours, it is rather difficult to find people who thrill with the blessings which have come to others; if a blessing does not benefit us, it is generally ignored. Every egotist wants to talk about his own operation. He has no time either to listen to the story of another person's illness, or to thank God for his own recovery. The egotists just want to boast about the length of their own incision, or how much money they inherited, or how many suits they own, or how many foxtails they have on their motorcycle.

Those of us who are obliged to read all the Psalms every week, and do it gladly, are often struck by the fact that the prayers of Israel were rather songs of praise than thanksgiving. This is because the Israelites were not individualistic; they were members of a mystical corporation of a religious nation, and nothing that was received by one was without a blessing to another. The individual Israelite inherited all that belonged to Israel. They rejoiced as the body rejoices. If the tongue tastes something sweet and delectable, the whole organism seems to echo and reverberate with the pleasure. No cell in the body has "fun" alone.

It would seem then that though thanksgiving or gratitude is noble, it was preceded historically by praise, as it is in children. More than that, it emphasized the charity, the brotherhood, the mutuality which binds men together. The Israelites instead of thanking for a favor, extended a blessing, as beggars are wont to do when they receive an alms. Every blessing brings God into it; every word of thanks does not.

Thus the noblest things in life have to be learned by effort, such as music and poetry. So does thanksgiving have to be taught to children, but even before they have learned to thank, they must learn to praise—to bless others and to praise God.

The Power of Love

THE MEANING OF LIFE

OUR DAILY EXPERIENCES are made up of a succession of television shows, a rapidity of newscasts interrupted by commercials, stop lights, and picture magazines.

The events of life are so cut up, isolated, fractioned, fissioned, atomized, so reduced to utter nakedness like architecture without decor, so condemned to mere factual, unrelated nothingness, that they quickly evaporate and dissolve. There is nothing that man carries away with him, except succession; there is the sunrise but no horizon, rivers but no beds, predicates but no subjects.

One can readily understand why Communism and Socialism have a strong political appeal to these de-personalized, dis-purposed creatures. Since they are no longer centers of responsibility, since their lives are without meaning, why not merge and mass them in a political collectivity? A totalitarian system is the forcible organization of a chaos created by the surrender of personal dignity and responsibility.

This fact is too obvious to merit development. What is more important is to suggest ways by which modern Humpty Dumpty may piece himself together and be a man. Here are some suggestions, not in the order of relative importance, but as the spirit moves.

1. No television show is worth seeing, no "views on the hour" is worth hearing, until one has found out the purpose of living. This purpose is related to happiness and not just a part of me, like the stomach, sex, and "left arm straight" when golfing. It is bound up with my desire for life, truth, and love. We can live without anything, except these three. What good is money without life? Why do I hate to have

secrets kept from me if I were not made to know truth—and not the truths of physics to the exclusion of philosophy, but all truth? What greater tragedy is there in life than to be unloved, except to live without showing love?

Would I want life or knowledge or love if they did not exist? Would I ever have eyes if there were no things to see? Does not the fraction of these desires for life and truth and love imply the whole? Would there be a shadow without light? The fact is I want Perfect Life, an all-embracing Knowledge, and Love without satiety and hate. This is the definition of God, Who is Father or Life, Who is the Word or Intelligence, Who is the Holy Spirit or Love.

2. To the degree that we fall away from this over-all purpose, we feel nauseated, unhappy, lost, and absurd. To the degree we return to it, we are happy and begin to love others.

3. Despite this knowledge of over-all purpose, each person can say: I am weak, since I resolve more than I do, since "the good which I will to do that I do not, and the evil which I will not, that I do." Hence there is need of outside help from the very Perfect Life, Truth, and Love I need for happiness. Because I feel like a watch which has all the parts, but with a main spring broken, I need repairs from the outside.

4. This outside Power illumines my mind in faith and strengthens my will in hope and love, if I accept it. But there is the "catch"—if I accept it. I cannot have it as long as I am selfish and sinful. I cannot serve God and Mammon.

5. Once I surrender the tinsel to have the jewel, then I enter into the mystery of love. I see that I do not love anyone unless he has some goodness in him, or is lovable in some way. But, I see also that God did not love me because I am lovable. I became lovable because God poured some of His Goodness and Love into me. I then begin to apply this charity to my neighbor. If I do not find him lovable, I put love into him as God puts Love into me, and thereby I provoke the response of love. Now, my personality is restored and I make the great discovery that no one is happy until he loves both God and neighbor.

THE ULTIMATE APPEAL TO VIRTUE

ONE OF the marks of decadence in society is the exaltation of little insignificant codes at the expense of great and eternal moral principles. As major morality weakens, minor morality strengthens. Dishpan hands in an advertising world are a greater tragedy than dishonest deeds. Codes are multiplied about the necessity of clean paper cups lest lips become polluted, but any censorship of garbage that enters the mind is looked upon as a restriction of freedom. Television sets moan the tragedy of a woman using a detergent soap which will make her sneeze; but the same television sets will carry in a single hour a threat or an act of violence every forty-five seconds. The sneeze must be prevented, but how few are concerned about preventing the violence seen on television from erupting in real life.

So it is with our little minor codes of ethics, with their little psychological maxims, such as "You must be integrated with yourself." But how can a broken pot mend itself? How can the blind lead the blind without both falling into the pit? Nor does it do any good to say: "You must be adjusted to your environment," when it is our environment that needs adjustment. How can one adjust oneself to a world that is full of wars and rumors of wars? Social environment does not know where it is going. It is made up of millions of little souls that are as changeable as weathercocks.

Society will never be made better until persons are better; persons will never be better until they have learned to love in the truest sense of the word. Where is the law that a daughter should love a mother? What rules govern friendship? Whenever a person is involved, we begin to see not mere duty, but the whole ensemble of relationships of life. How the life of a wicked person can be changed sometimes in the presence of a child, who passes not judgment on him! But somehow or other, the innocence of the child reminds him of the innocence that was once his and is now lost. As Francis Thompson put it in his poem "To Olivia":

> *Because thy arrows, not yet dire,*
> *Are still unbarbed with destined fire,*
> *I fear thee more than hadst thou stood*
> *Full-panoplied in womanhood.*

On a higher level, how often the self-indulgent character changes when he comes face to face with a person leading a life of sacrifice. Here there is an appeal to something that is dormant in every heart; the soul is stirred to its depths; tiny sparks under the ashes and the dust of years begin to be fanned into a flame; the spirit of sacrifice is appealed to in words which may never come to lips and yet which breathe: "I too would lead such a life. I would that I were like that."

The ultimate appeal to virtue, therefore, is not a code or a law, but a Person—a Person Who is at once Innocence and Self-Sacrificing. In the face of Divine Innocence and Sacrificial Love, no one can be sure of his holiness and his goodness. That is why each Apostle the night of the Last Supper asked, when Our Lord said that someone would betray Him: "Is it I, Lord?" They all knew in their hearts that they were capable of all manner of evil, but at the same time, they went forward to unmeasured gifts of sacrifice and devotion. In order to grow in truth and love, one must have personal truth and personal love—not mere abstractions. Furthermore, truth becomes lovable only when it is in flesh and blood. One cannot fall in love with a theorem of geometry, or a signpost on a roadway: "Thou shalt not exceed fifty miles an hour." Our Blessed Lord never said: "Follow this code," but "Follow Me . . . I am the way; I am truth and life."

THE MYSTERY OF SUFFERING

THE GREAT mystery of suffering will never be solved here below. At one moment, mankind came very close to having an explanation; that was when Job asked God many questions after his litany of woes. He had lost his children, his wife turned against him, he lost his fortune, and then his health. In despair, he began to ask heaven why he was born, why he ever saw the light of day, why he was ever nestled at his mother's breast. Finally God appears. If a Broadway dramatist were writing the play, he would either make God answer all the questions, or else he would keep on asking questions.

But when Infinite Wisdom appeared to Job, what actually happened was indeed strange. God, instead of answering the questions of Job, began to ask Job questions. They were all practical questions which belong within the range of astronomy, botany, biology, and zoology; in other words, questions of the natural order. When God finished asking Job questions, he understood that the questions of God were wiser than the answers of men. He saw that his intelligence was as nothing compared to the intelligence of God; that he no more understood the vast plan of the universe than a mouse nibbling the hammers on a piano can understand why anyone should disturb its peace by playing the keys. In the end Job received much more than he lost, for it is the last act that crowns the play.

In the light of eternity, suffering has a value not often dwelt upon. It sometimes supplies the defects of love. Man is made for perfect happiness, to be attained through loving Perfect Life, Perfect Truth, and Perfect Love. Most men settle for the shadow instead of the substance, the fraction instead of the whole, the temporal rather than the eternal, the carnal rather than the spiritual.

In transferring the infinite to the finite, man has the feeling that the world is too small for him; he is beating his wings against a cage; he has his feet in the mud and his mind in the stars. When golf bores him, he thinks of a trip to the moon. He would think an eagle foolish if it stayed in the dust staring at tinsel, yet he knows that is what he often does in his failure to aspire to the best and the highest.

What is at fault in the mind which accepts this ersatz happiness is really a defect of love. That is where suffering comes in; it compensates for the defects of love. God sometimes has to set fires under us to make us move, as a donkey driver puts nails in the back of the shaft to goad the stubbornness of the recalcitrant beast who backs up instead of going forward. It takes blows of the hammer and chisel to bring out the hidden form of marble; the violin strings would give forth uncertain sounds were there not a painful tightening to produce a perfect melody.

Franz Werfel wrote about sickness:

> The heedless and anarchic daily course of the sinner is subjected to a strict routine; the sinner is presented with a new childhood, and a new innocence, and not only through the penance which sickness exacts from him. His weakness deprives him of freedom and with it the opportunity of being the scoundrel that he is. Nature has temporarily arrested him in the Name of God, who knows whether he is already sitting in the death cell from which there is only a short way leading to the gallows, or whether he is simply detained for questioning and soon to be released again. In any case, no matter which is given, he has a chance to mend his ways.

Expressive of this idea is the poem of Richard Trench:

> *If there had anywhere appeared in space*
> *Another place of refuge, where to flee*
> *Our hearts had taken refuge in that place*
> *And not with Thee.*

*For we against creation's bars had beat
Like prisoner eagles, through great worlds had sought
Though but a foot of ground to plant our feet
Where Thou wert not.
And only when we found in earth and air
In Heaven or hell, that such might nowhere be
That we could not flee from Thee anywhere
We fled to Thee.*

THOSE WHO SUFFER PERSECUTION

"Blessed are you when all men speak well of you, when you are popular and in the limelight," is a beatitude of the world.

Let the Lord come into a world that believes that our whole life should be geared to flattering and influencing people for the sake of what they can do for us, and say to them: "Blessed are you when men hate you, persecute you, and revile you," and He will find Himself without a friend in the world, and an outcast on a hill with a mob shouting His death and His flesh hanging from Him like purple rags.

This Beatitude is really the Beatitude of the blessedness of being persecuted, or the happiness of being a martyr. In its full statement it runs: "Blessed are those who suffer persecution in the cause of right; the Kingdom of Heaven is theirs. Blessed are you, when men revile you, and persecute you, and speak all manner of evil against you falsely, because of Me. Be glad and lighthearted, for a rich reward awaits you in Heaven."

When Our Lord spoke of the world, He did not mean the physical world or the cosmos, He meant the spirit of the world which was arrayed against Him and His followers; a world which would one day kill his servants and think it was rendering a service to God, a world that is composed of human nature organizing itself against Divinity.

The Christian is bidden to be happy as Peter and the Apostles were when they were permitted to incorporate themselves to the Cross of Christ in order to share in the glory of His Resurrection. To be tolerated sometimes is a sign of weakness; to be persecuted is a compliment. The mediocre survive. The persecuted person shows that his belief is taken seriously and the cause for which he stands must be eliminated if evil is to conquer. True it is that evil men are persecuted, but they do not come within this Beatitude, for as Saint Paul said: "If I should deliver my body up to be burned and have not the love of God and neighbor in my heart, then it profits me nothing." A martyr must die for the faith, not for his property, nor his good name, nor for the sake of the Party. Self-made martyrs are numerous, but they have no place in the ranks of those who are promised the Kingdom of Heaven for taking the Cross of Christ on their shoulders.

One would expect that a person who is humble and unselfish, merciful and loving of mankind, should expect a peaceful end, but the Lord who made human hearts knew better. He, therefore, closed His Beatitudes by showing the treatment He would have us expect from the world.

Martyrs, witnesses to the Divine Love in the world, are promised the Kingdom of Heaven. They do not possess it merely because they suffer and endure; they rather suffer and endure because they already possess the Kingdom in their own hearts. One great and mysterious fact that is not generally known to the world is that wherever there is persecution on account of the Faith, it always results in a vast catch of souls for the Kingdom of God. Tertullian was right when he said: "Blood of the martyrs is the seed of the Church." The triumph of truth in Heaven is not enough; it must also have its glorious revenge in the very theater of its humiliations and conflicts. The world must see how mistaken it was in rejecting Divine Love, and must be forced to exclaim again with Julian the apostate: "Oh Galilean! Thou hast conquered!"

THE MEANING OF DEATH

DEATH IS an affirmation of the purpose of life in an otherwise meaningless existence. The world could carry on its Godless plan if there were no death. What death is to an individual, that catastrophe is to a civilization—the end of its wickedness. This is a source of anguish to the modern mind, for not only must man die, but the world must die. Death is a negative testimony to God's power in a meaningless world, for by it God brings meaningless existence to nought. Because God exists, evil cannot carry on its wickedness indefinitely. If there were no catastrophe, such as the Apocalypse reveals, at the end of the world, the universe would then be the triumph of chaos. But the catastrophe is a reminder that God will not allow unrighteousness to become eternal.

Death proves also that life has meaning, because it reveals that the virtues and goodness practiced within time do not find their completion except in eternity.

Man is much more afraid of dying in a train wreck or automobile accident than he is of dying on a battlefield or as a martyr to his faith. This proves that death is less terrifying and more meaningful when we rise above the level of the commonplace and lift ourselves into the realm of spiritual values.

That death is the end of evil is revealed too in the fact that the face of the dead is often more harmonious than the same face in life, as the sleeping face is more restful than the face awake. The ugly feelings and hates, eccentricities and discords, disappear in the presence of the dead, so much so that we use the expression, "Of the dead say nothing but good." In the face of the dead we give praise and adulation; we resurrect the good things and the charities, kindnesses and humor. All of these are recalled posthumously, making us wonder if death itself may not be the thrusting into the forefront of the good which we have done, rather than the evil. Not that both will not be recalled, but rather that as life brought out the debit side of our character, so death will also bring out the credit side. Death, in other words, is bound up with goodness.

Death is also bound up with love, or better, love is always bound up with death. He who accepts love accepts sacrifice. The ring of gold instead of the ring of tin is sacrifice, and sacrifice is a form of death. Beyond all of these minor sacrifices, the love is complete when it is most willing to accept for the beloved the sacrifice of death, as a soldier dies for his country. He who would attach too much value to life and run away from death, runs away from perfect love. "This is the greatest love a man can show, that he should lay down his life for his friends."

Death also will individualize and personalize us, who are today brought together in crowds and groups. Death separates the soul from the body; in doing so, each and every person is searched. Then shall be revealed my true self—not the self I think I am. The soul will stand naked before God as it truly is. If it is not clothed with virtue, it will feel ashamed as Adam and Eve did after their sin when they hid from God. It is curious that only after their sin did they feel naked and ashamed. The correlation between the nakedness of the soul and sin is manifested in the fact that the less people have of inner grace in this life, the more gaudily they dress; it is a kind of compensation for the nudity of their own souls. There shall then be only that *me* that sinned, that gave to the poor, that prayed, or that blasphemed. Then it will not be the *me* that lives, but the *me* that has lived, the *me* at the end of the day of life.

There will be no attorneys to plead the case, no alienists to argue that we were not in our right minds when we did wrong, there will be only one voice. It will be the voice of conscience which will reveal ourselves as we really are. We will thus be our own witness and our own judge. Nothing is as democratic as death—for in it, each man votes and decides his eternity.

THE RIGHT KIND OF OPTIMISM

It is not so much what happens to people that matters, but how they react to what happens. Two thieves were crucified on either side of Our Divine Lord. Both at first blasphemed, and yet one repented. There was some inflammable material in the soul of the thief at the right, which, when the spark of Divine Grace fell upon it, enkindled him to salvation.

One wonders if there was ever a more genuinely optimistic expression concerning even the ills of life than the words of Saint Paul: "We are well assured that everything helps to secure the good of those who love God." He does not say that every catastrophe and experience is good, for no one with faith would ever say that life does not have its miseries. Those who love react differently to the same affliction from those who love not. Love does not make a distinction between experiences on the basis of what is pleasant or profitable, but even can fit pain and conflict by the beautiful alchemy of love, to serve its own purposes and to give meaning to all of life's occurrences.

Here the true nature of faith appears; it is not an exalted state of feeling or an emotional persuasion, but rather an insight into the world as God has made it and the real purpose for which He uses it. A painful sickness borne with unmurmuring resignation to the loving Father Who sometimes gives out bitter medicine for a future good; the loss of property submitted to without any bitterness because of a knowledge that we have a higher treasure; the loss of a loved one impressing upon the soul that all the love we have on this earth is but a spark from the Flame, Which is God—all these trials enter into the fabric of the mantle of sanctity for those who have faith. There is good which comes out of things even when there is no good in them.

The old Stoics used to say: "Grit your teeth; submit to fate," recommending that in the face of any trial one take an icy, scornful attitude. The Epicureans recommended: "Make yourself insensible to pain by indulgence in pleasure." But here the recommendation is to discover a wise and loving God directing all the mixed processes of life to a beneficent issue. Thus it soothes the heart into patience, lifts it into hope, and floods it with courage. As the rainbow would never be seen if it were not for the clouds and the rain, so, too, the beauty of holiness would never shine so brightly were it not for the trials which the Spirit of God employs to promote them. It is the winds and the winters which try the herbs, the flowers, and the trees; only the strongest survive. Likewise, tribulation tries the soul, and in the strong it develops patience, and patience in its turn, hope, and hope finally begets love.

Outward attacks and troubles rather fix than unsettle a man with true faith, as tempests from without only serve to root the oak deeper into the ground. But an inward canker will gradually rot and decay it. The big problem facing every man is whether he will, under difficulties, ride out the storm to port. If he knows why he is living, then he will substitute the one great consuming purpose for his tiny little wishes, and thus make life happy.

OTHER IMAGE BOOKS

ABANDONMENT TO DIVINE PROVIDENCE – Jean Pierre de Caussade. Trans. by John Beevers

AGING: THE FULFILLMENT OF LIFE – Henri J. M. Nouwen and Walter J. Gaffney

AND WOULD YOU BELIEVE IT – Bernard Basset, S.J.

APOLOGIA PRO VITA SUA – John Henry Cardinal Newman

AN AQUINAS READER – Ed., with an Intro., by Mary T. Clark

THE ART OF BEING HUMAN – William McNamara, O.C.D.

ASCENT OF MOUNT CARMEL – St. John of the Cross – Trans. and ed. by E. Allison Peers

AN AUGUSTINE READER – Ed., with an Intro., by John J. O'Meara

AUTOBIOGRAPHY OF ST. THÉRÈSE OF LISIEUX: THE STORY OF A SOUL – A new translation by John Beevers

BELIEVING – Eugene Kennedy

CATHOLIC AMERICA – John Cogley

THE CHALLENGE OF JESUS – John Shea

CHRIST IS ALIVE! – Michel Quoist

CHRIST THE LORD – Gerard S. Sloyan

THE CHURCH – Hans Küng

CITY OF GOD – St. Augustine – Ed. by Vernon J. Bourke. Intro. by Étienne Gilson

THE CLOUD OF UNKNOWING (and THE BOOK OF PRIVY COUNSELING) – Newly ed., with an Intro., by William Johnston, S.J.

THE CONFESSIONS OF ST. AUGUSTINE – Trans., with an Intro., by John K. Ryan

CONJECTURES OF A GUILTY BYSTANDER – Thomas Merton

THE CONSPIRACY OF GOD: THE HOLY SPIRIT IN US – John C. Haughey

CONTEMPLATION IN A WORLD OF ACTION – Thomas Merton

CONTEMPLATIVE PRAYER – Thomas Merton

CREATIVE MINISTRY – Henri J. M. Nouwen

DAMIEN THE LEPER – John Farrow

DARK NIGHT OF THE SOUL – St. John of the Cross. Ed. and trans. by E. Allison Peers

THE DEVIL YOU SAY! – Andrew M. Greeley

THE DIARY OF A COUNTRY PRIEST – Georges Bernanos

DIVORCE AND REMARRIAGE FOR CATHOLICS? – Stephen J. Kelleher

A DOCTOR AT CALVARY – Pierre Barbet, M.D.

EVERLASTING MAN – G. K. Chesterton

A FAMILY ON WHEELS: FURTHER ADVENTURES OF THE TRAPP FAMILY SINGERS – Maria Augusta Trapp with Ruth T. Murdoch

FIVE FOR SORROW, TEN FOR JOY – J. Neville Ward

OTHER IMAGE BOOKS

THE FOUR GOSPELS: AN INTRODUCTION (2 vols.) – Bruce Vawter, C.M.

THE FREEDOM OF SEXUAL LOVE – Joseph and Lois Bird

THE FRIENDSHIP GAME – Andrew M. Greeley

A GOOD MAN IS HARD TO FIND – Flannery O'Connor

THE GOSPELS AND THE JESUS OF HISTORY – Xavier Léon-Dufour, S.J.

THE GREATEST STORY EVER TOLD – Fulton Oursler

GUIDE TO CONTENTMENT – Fulton J. Sheen

GUILTY, O LORD – Bernard Basset, S.J.

HEART IN PILGRIMAGE – Evelyn Eaton and Edward Roberts Moore

HE LEADETH ME – Walter J. Ciszek, S.J., with Daniel Flaherty, S.J.

HINDU THEOLOGY: A READER – Ed. by José Pereira

A HISTORY OF PHILOSOPHY: VOLUME 1 – GREECE AND ROME (2 Parts) – Frederick Copleston, S.J.

A HISTORY OF PHILOSOPHY: VOLUME 2 – MEDIAEVAL PHILOSOPHY (2 Parts) – Frederick Copleston, S.J. Part I – Augustine to Bonaventure. Part II – Albert the Great to Duns Scotus

A HISTORY OF PHILOSOPHY: VOLUME 3 – LATE MEDIAEVAL AND RENAISSANCE PHILOSOPHY (2 Parts) – Frederick Copleston, S.J. Part I – Ockham to the Speculative Mystics. Part II – The Revival of Platonism to Suárez

A HISTORY OF PHILOSOPHY: VOLUME 4 – MODERN PHILOSOPHY: Descartes to Leibniz – Frederick Copleston, S.J.

A HISTORY OF PHILOSOPHY: VOLUME 5 – MODERN PHILOSOPHY: The British Philosophers, Hobbes to Hume (2 Parts) – Frederick Copleston, S.J. Part I – Hobbes to Paley. Part II – Berkeley to Hume

A HISTORY OF PHILOSOPHY: VOLUME 6 – MODERN PHILOSOPHY (2 Parts) – Frederick Copleston, S.J. – The French Enlightenment to Kant

A HISTORY OF PHILOSOPHY: VOLUME 7 – MODERN PHILOSOPHY (2 Parts) – Frederick Copleston, S.J. Part I – Fichte to Hegel. Part II – Schopenhauer to Nietzsche

A HISTORY OF PHILOSOPHY: VOLUME 8 – MODERN PHILOSOPHY: Bentham to Russell (2 Parts) – Frederick Copleston, S.J. Part I – British Empiricism and the Idealist Movement in Great Britain. Part II – Idealism in America, the Pragmatist Movement, the Revolt against Idealism

A HISTORY OF PHILOSOPHY: VOLUME 9 – Maine de Biran to Sartre (2 Parts) – Frederick Copleston, S.J. Part I – The Revolution to Henri Bergson. Part II – Bergson to Sartre